706

Smart Economics

Smart Economics

*Commonsense Answers to 50
Questions about Government,
Taxes, Business, and Households*

MICHAEL L. WALDEN

Westport, Connecticut
London

Library of Congress Cataloging-in-Publication Data

Walden, M. L. (Michael Leonard), 1951–
  Smart economics : commonsense answers to 50 questions about government, taxes, business, and households / Michael L. Walden.
    p. cm.
  Includes bibliographical references and index.
  ISBN 0–275–98750–7 (alk. paper)
    1. United States—Economic policy—2001– 2. Fiscal policy—United States. 3. Government spending policy—United States. I. Title.
  HC106.83.W35 2005
  336.3'0973—dc22   2005013509

British Library Cataloguing in Publication Data is available.

Library of Congress Catalog Card Number: 2005013509
ISBN: 0–275–98750–7

First published in 2005

Praeger Publishers, 88 Post Road West, Westport, CT 06881
An imprint of Greenwood Publishing Group, Inc.
www.praeger.com

Printed in the United States of America

The paper used in this book complies with the Permanent Paper Standard issued by the National Information Standards Organization (Z39.48–1984).

10 9 8 7 6 5 4 3 2 1

■ Contents ■

Introduction   ix

I. Economic Questions about What Government Does, What Government Doesn't Do, and How Government Spends Our Money

  1. Has Government Growth Been Out of Control?   3

  2. Will the National Debt Sink Our Economic Future?   6

  3. Do Budget Deficits Increase Interest Rates?   10

  4. Can Government Spending Be Cut by Eliminating Waste?   14

  5. Does Government Spend Too Much, or Not Enough, on the Poor?   17

  6. Does War Help the Economy?   21

  7. Does More Spent on Education Pay Off in Student Achievement?   24

  8. Has the Social Security Surplus Been Stolen?   27

  9. Is Social Security Going Bankrupt?   30

10. Should Our Money Be Backed by Gold?   34

11. Should Government Enforce a Living Wage?   37

12. Should Government Control the Prices of Necessities?   39

13. Should Government Pay Businesses to Create Jobs?   43

14. Can Government Create Prosperity?   46

Contents

II. Economic Questions about How Much Taxes Are Paid, Who Pays Taxes, and the Fairness of Taxes

15. Do We Pay 60% to 80% of Our Income in Taxes?   51

16. Does a Tax Bracket of 40% Mean the Government Takes 40% of Your Income?   55

17. Can Cutting Tax Rates Increase Tax Revenues?   59

18. Will a Tax Cut of $1 Create $7 to $10 of New Income?   62

19. Do Corporations Pay Too Little in Taxes?   65

20. Would Rich Investors Benefit from a Flat Tax?   68

21. Is the Sales Tax Regressive?   70

22. Do the Rich Get a Break on Social Security Taxes?   73

23. Has the Tax Penalty for Marriage Been Ended?   75

III. Economic Questions about What Business Does and Why and How That Affects Jobs, Consumers, and the Country

24. Is American Manufacturing Dying?   81

25. Are Low-Paying Jobs Replacing High-Paying Ones?   84

26. Are Companies Outsourcing Good-Paying Jobs?   87

27. Will Free Trade Destroy Our Economy?   92

28. Can U.S. Workers Compete with Low-Paid Foreign Workers?   96

29. Do Countries Prosper Only If They Run a Trade Surplus?   99

30. Is a "Strong" Dollar Good and a "Weak" Dollar Bad?   102

31. Are Profits Bad?   105

32. Does Business Make Obscene Profits?   110

33. Does Big Business Control the Economy?   113

34. Can Pro Sports Teams and Facilities Hit Economic Home Runs?   116

35. Why Are Pro Sports Stars Paid So Much for
    Playing a Game?   119

36. Are We Running Out of Farmers, Farmland,
    and Soon, Food?   123

37. Are Gas Prices at an All-Time High?   126

38. Do Big Oil Companies Manipulate Oil Supplies and
    Gas Prices?   130

39. Should We Become Energy Self-Sufficient?   133

40. Is Immigration Hurting Our Economy?   136

IV. Economic Questions about How Households Live and How They Earn and Spend Money

41. Is Everything More Expensive Today (or, Should You
    Wish for the "Good Old Days")?   141

42. Does It Take Two Incomes for Families to
    Get Ahead Today?   143

43. Are Americans Drowning in Debt and Not Saving?   148

44. Do Women Earn Less Than Men?   153

45. Are the Rich Getting Richer and Everyone Else
    Getting Poorer?   156

46. Is Poverty Getting Worse?   160

47. If It Saves One Life, Is It Worth the Cost?   164

48. Can Families Afford College?   167

49. Would Importing Drugs Lower Their Prices?   171

50. Can Government Lower Consumers' Health Costs?   175

Glossary   179

Notes   185

Index   203

■ Introduction ■

Everywhere you turn, there's economics. Whether it's talk around the office watercooler, chatting over the neighbor's fence, or discussion on talk radio, you just can't get away from economics. The economic content may not jump out, but it's there, nevertheless.

The reason is simple. Economics is at the heart of so much of what we talk about because economics underlies our daily decisions over how to use resources. In fact, the only reason economics as a discipline was invented was to help people make the best decisions regarding the use of their limited resources. You've heard the phrase "You can't have it all." Well, much as we'd like to, we can't. There are many competing uses for our time and money; economics is there to help us make choices.

So it's not surprising to hear and read about economics every day. Just look at a typical serving of topics on talk radio. Government actions and government spending are favorite "hot-button" topics, with issues like government waste, Social Security, the budget deficit, a living wage, and business incentives. Taxes are always a come-on, and the weekly roster of tax issues might be who pays taxes, how much taxes are paid, and the impact of tax cuts.

Business isn't ignored on the radio gabfest, with headline-grabbing topics like "obscene" profits, salaries of CEOs (chief executive officers) and professional athletes, outsourcing, and oil and gas prices. And household economic issues certainly get coverage, such as incomes of the rich and poor, poverty, debt loads, college expenses, and prescription drug prices.

To an economist (which I am), the pervasiveness of economic discussions is heartening. But it's also frustrating and troubling because so much of the discussion is just plain wrong and misleading.

There are two reasons for this. One is time. We live in a fast-paced society where everything must be condensed in time. Names are shortened to one syllable, and entire paragraphs are summarized in one phrase.

So it's not surprising that economic issues become abbreviated. For example: Government spending is wasteful, taxes are too high, good-paying jobs are being shipped overseas, American manufacturing is dead, and Americans don't save. These shorthands give the benefit and security of presenting both the issue and conclusion in one compact statement.

Second, many economic issues have become hijacked by political partisans (on both the Left and Right) who have a predetermined point of view. So we hear: "Tax cuts pay for themselves," "trade must be fair," and "service jobs pay less than manufacturing positions." These partisans aren't interested in explaining and understanding the issue. They're only interested in using the issue to advance an agenda.

The goal of this book is simple: Take fifty of today's top economic issues and explain their meaning, implications, and potential solutions (where they exist) in a logical, straightforward, commonsense, and nonpartisan way. I use economic concepts and evidence in presenting the issues. But don't worry—you'll find no equations and only simple graphs; plus, no background in economics is required.

I do copy one characteristic from the common coverage of economic issues—brevity. In order to compete for your limited time, the fifty chapters are short and to the point—yet they should open your eyes to the *Smart* way of viewing today's economy.

The book is divided into four parts: economic questions about government, about taxes, about business, and about households. Each chapter is self-contained, so you can skip ahead to any question you desire. Hopefully you'll learn a new way—the *Smart* way—of looking at economic issues, and you'll absorb some economics as a bonus!

 Economic Questions about What Government Does, What Government Doesn't Do, and How Government Spends Our Money

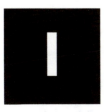

Has Government Growth Been Out of Control?

In 2003, government at all levels in the United States spent $3.5 billion. By contrast, all governments in the United States spent $116 billion in 1959.[1] So the increase in government spending from 1959 to 2003 was a whopping 3,017%!

Clearly this means government has grown enormously and is out of control, right? Not necessarily.

First, in economics we can never compare past dollar amounts to present dollar amounts. Because prices were generally lower in earlier years, past dollars went further—they bought more—than current dollars. So we must always adjust dollars in different years for their different "purchasing power."

When this is done, a slightly different picture emerges. Government spending has increased, but not as much as at first glance. The increase from 1959 to 2003 was 377%.[2] This is a more modest increase but an increase nevertheless.

But two other factors complicate the issue. Population has increased over time, and it makes sense government spending would increase as population increases.

Also, along with population growth has occurred income growth. More income likely means more government spending on roads, defense, public safety, and so on, as more commerce is taking place.

To look at the impacts of population and income growth on government spending, we can compare two measures: government spending per person adjusted for purchasing power of the dollar (Figure 1, solid line, in thousands of 2003 purchasing power dollars) and government spending as a percentage of national income (Figure 1, dashed line).

Both measures show government spending has increased, but not at breakneck speed. Indeed, as measured by the percentage of national in-

FIGURE I. A More Modest Increase in Government

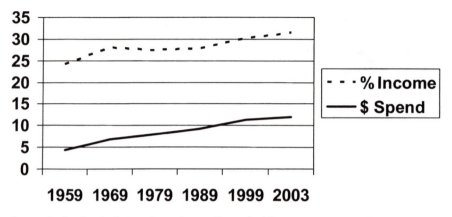

Source: Author's calculations from data in Council of Economic Advisors, *Economic Report of the President, 2004.*

come taken, government spending has hovered between 25% and 30% of total income in the country during the past forty-five years. Government spending per person, adjusted for the dollar's purchasing power, has increased 180% since 1959. Surely this is an increase, but it's much less than the whopping 3,000% jump reported at the start of this chapter.

But I'm not finished, because there's another wrinkle to the story. Government spending can be broadly divided into two parts: (1) spending on services provided by government, like defense, public safety, roads, courts, and K–12 schools, and (2) spending on the transfer of money or money-like resources to various groups of citizens, including programs like Social Security, Medicare, Medicaid, and welfare programs.

The two types of spending are fundamentally different. Government spending on services means government is actually doing something—like building or maintaining a road, guarding our national interests, catching criminals, and teaching children in the public schools—and most of us benefit from these services. Government spending on transfers means the government is providing income or paying for a particular kind of spending, like medical care, and only those who directly receive the income or have a cost paid beg the benefit of the transfers.

If government spending on services as a percentage of national income and government spending on transfers as a percentage of national income are compared, an amazing difference is seen. Government spending on transfers has more than doubled from 1959 to 2003 (4.9% to 12.4%), while government spending on services has actually declined (16.4% to 15.5%).[3] If the 16.4% rate had been maintained in 2003, it would have resulted in $100 billion more spent on government services. It's no wonder that many people think government is doing less while costing more. People see relatively less government services like police, roads, and teachers. But they don't see the increased government transfers unless they're directly on the receiving end.

Smart Economics looks beyond the scary headlines of increases in government spending and understands several adjustments must be made to compare government spending trends over time. When these adjustments are made, two conclusions are reached. Relative to the size of national income, government provision of services has fallen, whereas government programs that transfer spending power among citizens have expanded. In the past quarter century, government at all levels has been spending between 25 and 30 cents of every dollar of income in the economy.

2 Will the National Debt Sink Our Economic Future?

At the end of 2003 the national debt stood at $7 trillion.[1] This is the amount of money the federal government owes, like the home mortgage or car loan most families have. The difference is the federal government won't help you and me pay our mortgage and car loan, whereas we, the taxpayers, are the only source for paying the national debt.

The national debt is one of those issues on which some on both the Right and the Left agree. They agree it should be reduced, if not totally paid off. They cite a number of ills from the national debt: a drag on the economy, a burden for our children and grandchildren, high interest rates, and maybe even high blood pressure from worrying about the debt.

But like most hype about the national economy, hand-wringing over the national debt suffers from ignorance about the proper way to measure it and about its meaning.

Let's tackle measurement first. Sure, $7 trillion is a big number. Debt worriers are fond of calculating how many times around the earth or trips to the moon stringing 7 billion dollar bills would make. Or they like to show a sharply rising graph of the rising national debt from Revolutionary War days to today.

But although these measures of the national debt may be mind-boggling, they are really worthless. Let me ask you a question. If I asked how much debt you had and you said $100,000, could I automatically conclude you were about to declare bankruptcy? Why, of course not. Debt of $100,000 to someone earning $10,000 a year would be a problem. But debt of $100,000 to someone earning $500,000 annually would be no big deal.

So in measuring the size of debt, whether it is the national debt or the Smith family's debt, what matters is the size of the debt relative to the ability to pay the debt—usually measured by annual income. In 2001, the average American family had a debt to income ratio of 89%, meaning the family had debt equal to 89% of their annual income.[2] And guess what? The national debt as a percentage of national income in 2003 was less, at 63%![3] Furthermore, this national debt to income ratio is not an all-time high, and it is actually lower than the national debt ratios in many foreign countries.[4]

Does this mean we don't have to worry about the national debt? Of course we do. We should monitor the national debt ratio and particularly worry if it rises when the economy is growing and the nation is at peace. It is typical for the national debt ratio to rise during two times: when the nation is at war and when the economy is in recession. So, for example, the national debt ratio rose in 2001 and 2002 when the economy was in recession and when both the war on terrorism and the buildup to the Iraqi war were occurring. During the 1990s, when the nation was at relative peace and the economy was growing, the national debt ratio fell.

But there's no need to get hysterical about the national debt. Rather than focusing on the scary dollar amount, keep your eye on the national debt to income ratio. And remember, just like most households and businesses will carry debt, so too will most governments.

This leads to the second issue, the meaning of the national debt. Why should governments be in debt at all? Wouldn't the best government be one that had no debt? And what about this idea—why not have the government simply cancel its debt and start from scratch?

Wait a minute! I bet if you really knew to whom the government owes the debt, you'd quickly sour on any idea of canceling the national debt. The fact is the majority of the national debt is owed to you and me. If you have any direct investments in U.S. government Treasury securities, or if the mutual funds you're invested in hold some U.S. government Treasury securities (as is quite common), then you are a holder of some of the national debt. Some people mistakenly think most of the national debt is owed to foreigners. Not so! Foreigners own about 25% of the total U.S. national debt.[5]

But if canceling the national debt is a bad idea, shouldn't we pressure governments to get away from using debt and to move totally to a "pay as you go" basis? Shouldn't governments, as well as families, follow the recommendation of my mother, "Don't buy it unless you have the cash"?

Although I loved my late mother, she was wrong about always advising against borrowing. If governments were forced to pay for things only from current revenues, this could actually wreak havoc with family finances.

Here's why. Say a local government needs to build new schools because the number of children in the area is increasing. Say the construction of the schools will cost $200 million and take one year. If the government was forced to "pay as you go" with only current tax revenues, it would have to jack up tax rates in this one year. Taxpayers in this one year would be forced to totally pay for the schools even though future taxpayers would benefit from having the schools.

Wouldn't a better way be to have all taxpayers who reap rewards from the new schools pay for them? This can happen by having the government borrow the $200 million to build the schools now and then have the loan repaid in the future. In this way the school buildings would be financed and paid for while children are being educated in the buildings. And this method would avoid having taxpayers in one year overburdened by footing the entire bill for the schools.

The logic of this method of financing the school buildings is the same as the logic most families use to purchase a home. If most of us waited to buy a home with cash (as my mother would have recommended), then few of us would ever be homeowners. But by borrowing the money, we can buy a home and pay for it while we're enjoying it. This makes eminent economic sense.

Corporations do the same thing. If General Motors decides to build a new auto factory, they'll likely borrow the money, build the plant, and pay for the plant with some of the money earned by manufacturing vehicles in the factory.

Some of you may still not like borrowing, because borrowing costs more when interest is included than if the school buildings, home, or auto factory were paid for all at once with cash. For example, even with a modest interest rate of 4.5%, borrowing a dollar and repaying it over fifteen years will cost one-third more than just paying that dollar today.

If you think this way, you've fallen into the trap of treating future dollars like current dollars. But they're not the same because of one simple fact: inflation. A dollar in fifteen years is only like 64 cents today when the annual inflation rate is 3%. So sure, you'll pay more total dollars when borrowing than when paying with cash today, but the *purchasing power* of those payments is much closer.

So here's what all of this means for government borrowing. Similar to families and companies, government borrowing makes sense when the government is funding a large, long-lasting project that will benefit taxpayers many years in the future. In this case it makes perfect sense for the government to borrow the money, build the project, and spread the payments into the future to taxpayers who enjoy the benefits of the project.

In fact, this kind of thinking is so sensible that most local and state governments take a cue from companies and keep two budgets, a capital budget and an operating budget. The capital budget is specifically for the kind of large, long-lasting projects described above, like roads, sewers, bridges, buildings, and other infrastructure. Borrowing is allowed—and indeed, expected—in the capital budget. The operating budget is for all other kinds of government spending, including salaries for government workers, and the operating budget must be balanced each year with no borrowing.

Unfortunately, the federal government's budgetary process doesn't follow this kind of logic. All types of federal spending are lumped into one budget. Economists and accountants have long thought the federal budget would be much more sensible if it was divided into a capital budget and an operating budget. The capital budget would include spending for items like roads, bridges, and military hardware (tanks, aircraft carriers, jet fighters), and funds for this spending could be borrowed. The federal operating budget would include spending for the day-to-day operations of the government, and this budget would have to be balanced except in times of war or recession.

Smart Economics doesn't fall for the doomsday warnings about federal borrowing and the national debt. When put in the context of our total national income, the national debt is manageable. *Smart Economics* also recognizes there are both time periods and spending programs for which government borrowing makes absolute sense. Greater logic could be added to the federal government's budgetary process if the feds followed the lead of local and state governments and of the corporate world and maintained two budgets—one for reasonable borrowing and the other balanced for operating expenditures.

Do Budget Deficits Increase Interest Rates?

3

The political winds swirling around budget deficits have shifted during the past seventy years. In the 1930s, Democrats championed budget deficits as a way for the federal government to spend money and jump-start the economy during recessions. Republicans called such budget deficits fiscally irresponsible.

But after 1980, the positions shifted. First under Ronald Reagan in the 1980s, and then under George Bush and George W. Bush, large budget deficits occurred under Republican presidents. Republicans said the deficits had no negative impacts on the economy and maybe even helped by restraining government spending. Democrats smiled and said the deficits were the height of fiscal irresponsibility and harmed the economy.

What harm could deficits do to the economy? One of the main worries is they increase interest rates. In fact, the budget deficit and interest rate connection is virtually accepted as "fact" by the media, businesspersons, and persons on the street.

The argument is this: When the government runs a budget deficit, the government must borrow money to finance it. So bigger budget deficits mean more government borrowing. The government borrowing competes with borrowing by businesses and households (in economics lingo, the "demand" for borrowing increases). And, as when more people want to buy apples, when the combined borrowing by the government, businesses, and households increases, the "price" of borrowing—the interest rate—rises.

I have to be honest here. This is a very reasonable explanation. And it's not really silly to think budget deficits cause interest rates to rise. Many economics textbooks bluntly state this as fact.[1]

So why would I question the claim of a tie between budget deficits and interest rates? Because it is stated by many believers with no questions asked. It's simply accepted as a "matter of fact" that when budget deficits increase, so too do interest rates.

But this "fact" simply isn't the case after examining the evidence. Look at Figures 2 and 3. They show the relationship between short-term interest rates (Figure 2) and long-term interest rates (Figure 3) and budget deficits. Budget deficits are properly measured as a percentage of national income, with the one year when a budget surplus occurred (1999) indicated by a negative number. Interest rates have been adjusted to remove inflation, since the inflation rate incorporated in interest rates does not represent a real return to lending (this is called the *real* interest rate).

Although both figures show some years when interest rates rose as budget deficits rose (early 1980s), the figures also show periods when in-

FIGURE 2. Budget Deficits and Short-Term Interest Rates

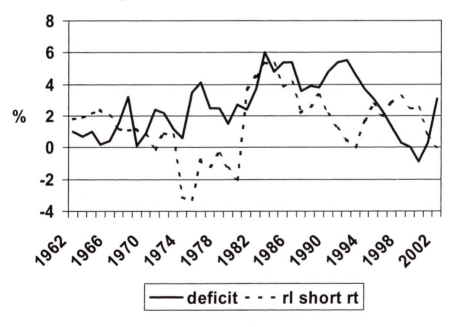

The short-term interest rate is the three-month Treasury bill rate minus the consumer price index (CPI) inflation rate; the deficit is the budget deficit divided by gross domestic product (GDP).

Sources: Council of Economic Advisors, *Economic Report of the President, 2004*; Federal Reserve System, "Recent Changes."

FIGURE 3. Budget Deficits and Long-Term Interest Rates

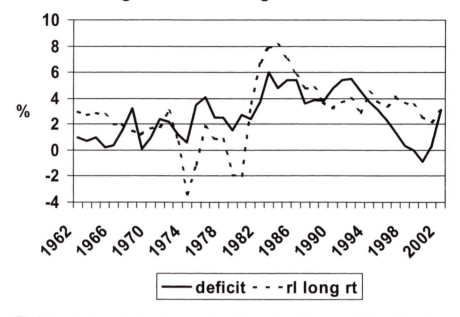

The long-term interest rate is the ten-year Treasury bond rate minus the CPI inflation rate; the deficit is the budget deficit divided by GDP.

Sources: Council of Economic Advisors, *Economic Report of the President, 2004*; Federal Reserve System, "Recent Changes."

terest rates changed little as budget deficits shifted (mid-1990s) and periods when interest rates fell as deficits increased (2000–2003). In fact, a large number of economic studies on this subject applying very sophisticated statistical techniques have *not* found a link between budget deficits and interest rates.[2]

How can this be? There are two explanations. First, many, many, many factors affect the level of interest rates, including, but not limited to, the growth of money and credit, foreign exchange rates (how many U.S. dollars can be traded for foreign currency), forecasts of future economic growth, national and worldwide fears and uncertainties, business and consumer confidence, and politics. Any impacts budget deficits might have on interest rates can be swamped by these other factors.

Second, in the story (six paragraphs above) explaining why bigger budget deficits lead to higher interest rates, there was an assumption that borrowing by businesses and households wouldn't change when government borrowing (to fund the deficit) increased.

Actually, a case can be made that business and household borrowing declines when government borrowing increases. The reason is that when government borrowing increases, businesses and households anticipate the government will have to increase taxes in the future to pay off the loans. So businesses and households borrow less and save more today in order to meet their higher future tax bills, and this behavior keeps interest rates stable when government borrows more.

I know many of you think this explanation is foolish. Yet economists have actually found support for this explanation going back as long as 250 years.[3]

Don't get me wrong. There's plenty to worry about with budget deficits, such as what they imply for the size of government and the amount of tax bills down the road. And economists will continue to argue about any possible link between budget deficits, or *forecasts* of budget deficits, and the level of interest rates.[4] But the claim that higher budget deficits lead to higher interest rates is far from a "slam dunk."

Smart Economics knows the link between budget deficits and interest rates is weak, at best. Interest rates are determined by a whole boatload of factors. There are times when interest rates have risen when budget deficits have turned to surpluses, and vice versa. You'll make a big mistake if you try to forecast the direction of interest rates by movements in the federal budget deficit.

4 Can Government Spending Be Cut by Eliminating Waste?

Here's the deal. You decide to run for political office. It really doesn't matter if it's a local, state, or federal office, and it doesn't matter what political party, if any, you're attached to. You meet with your political advisers to decide on a platform. One of the advisers raises her hand and says: "Be against government waste. Say you will reduce government spending without reducing services by cutting out waste." No one disagrees. After all, who could? Like mom and apple pie, everyone from across the political spectrum is for eliminating wasteful government spending.

But where in any government budget is a line item labeled "waste"? Unless it's short for "waste collection," you won't find it.

But surely, you say, there are many wasteful government *programs*, meaning programs that don't accomplish much. Although this may be true, here's the rub. One person's wasteful government program is another person's necessary and productive program. In fact, if a government program didn't have backers, it wouldn't exist. There's an old joke that says only rocks and dirt are older than government programs. Because every government program has supporters and constituents, once a program is established, it's hard to eliminate.

Even government programs that serve very few people are hard to cut. Take farm subsidies, which cost the federal government $20 billion annually.[1] Farmers comprise less than 2% of the population.[2] Much of the farm subsidies go to large, corporate farms,[3] and studies have shown farm subsidies generally lead to higher food prices for consumers.[4] Yet farmers have been able to amass enough political clout to keep farm subsidies in the federal budget.

Political candidates are also fond of saying they will run government like a business, and this will reduce waste. But it's precisely because government *can't* be run like a business that means we will always have some degree of "wasteful" government spending.

Here's what I mean. The objective of a business is very simple—make the biggest profit possible. Everything in a business is geared to maximizing profit. Managers and workers are always on the lookout for expenses that aren't generating profit. For example, say a business is running a radio advertisement costing $5,000 a month. By interviewing customers, the business determines the ads only bring in $3,000 of monthly sales. Because the ads have a negative profit ($3,000 sales − $5,000 costs = −$2,000 profit), the business will discontinue the radio spots.

But suppose the government runs ads encouraging people not to drink when they drive. Will the ads ever be judged by their profitability? No, because there's no profit to be calculated. At best, government bureaucrats will try to determine if the incidence of drunken driving falls when the ads are running. And you know what—I'll bet they'll find it! In fact, some statement like, "If the ads prevent just *one* drunken driving accident, they're worth it" will likely be made. Since the bureaucrats' jobs are based, in part, on this kind of government spending, the government workers have a natural incentive to keep the spending going.

In short, you need to realize the objective of government is *not* to make a profit. Most government services and programs don't earn money, so calculating a profit isn't even possible. The objective of most government programs is to serve the most people possible, and the more people served, the more costly the program. So by government logic, the more costly the program and the bigger the budget, the more successful the government program!

So are government bureaucrats dishonest people who are purposefully trying to bankrupt the taxpayer? Not at all. Government bureaucrats respond to the incentives they confront just like businesspersons. If the incentive of businesspersons is to make a profit, then everything they do will be motivated by the profit objective. But if the incentive before government bureaucrats is to serve as many people as possible and spend all this year's budget so they'll get a bigger budget next year, then this is what they'll do.

OK, so the government is not in the profit-making business. But can't government workers still be given an incentive to worry about efficiency? Can't government bureaucrats be given an incentive to worry about costs per person served, with the objective of keeping costs per person served low? If $1 million is spent in radio ads to prevent one drunk driving accident, shouldn't there be an evaluation as to whether this is the best way to reduce drunk driving?

Sure, but then there will likely be complaints from the clients (the persons served) of the government program. If drunk driving ads are eliminated, MADD (Mothers against Drunk Driving) will say the government is uncaring and not serious about reducing drunk driving accidents. Or take the example of Medicare, the multi-hundred-billion-dollar federal medical program for the elderly. Periodically the government has imposed rules to increase the efficiency of the program, such as limiting hospital stays and requiring benefit/cost analysis of drug treatments. Predictably, an outcry arises about the alleged "insensitivity" and "unfairness" of the changes, and often the government retracts the rules.

So does all this mean we have to give up on the goal of reducing government waste? No, but we have to be more realistic in thinking wasteful government spending can easily be eliminated. Two tactics should be followed for reducing government waste.

First, recognize that government workers and program managers respond to incentives just like workers in the private sector. So institute financial rewards for government bureaucrats who reduce program costs as long as program quality and client satisfaction are maintained. This is a goal of any private company—to deliver the same product or service at a lower cost—and as taxpayers, we'd like the government to do the same. So if the government wants to reduce drunk driving, financially reward government bureaucrats who are able to show their program results in more reductions in drunk driving per dollar spent than alternative programs.

Second, where practical, consider the privatization of government programs. Privatization means the government still pays for the program, but the program is *delivered* by a private firm. The government takes bids from private firms for running the program and chooses the firm with the lowest bid. However, the contract with the private firm is for a limited time period, and the government would closely monitor and measure program quality and client satisfaction. Yet competition between firms for the government contract is a motivation to eliminate wasteful spending.

Smart Economics recognizes that reducing wasteful government spending is easier said than done. Since every government program has a supporting constituency, it's virtually impossible to eliminate any program completely. To reduce waste internally, government workers must be given a clear financial incentive to do so. Also, having private companies compete for managing and operating government programs is another way to improve the effectiveness and efficiency of government spending.

Does Government Spend Too Much, or Not Enough, on the Poor?

Spending on the poor is, perhaps next to taxes, where the biggest split exists between the Right and the Left. Simply put, the Right claims too much is spent on the poor, and the Left says not enough is spent.

This disagreement can be easily answered by checking the numbers. Each year the federal government compiles the *Green Book*, a summary of all government programs that transfer resources among citizens. The latest data (for 2002) show $522 billion was spent by federal, state, and local governments on various programs to help the poor (technically called *income-tested* programs).[1] Here's how the spending breaks down:

Medical	$283 billion
Cash	$102 billion
Food	$39 billion
Housing	$36 billion
Education	$30 billion
Services	$22 billion
Job training	$8 billion
Energy	$2 billion[2]

Now, right off the bat you can see $522 billion is not a small amount of money. But as I've emphasized several times, large amounts of money must always be put in perspective. So to know if $522 billion is a large, moderate, or small amount of spending on the poor, we need to spread the total over the number of folks classified as poor.

There are two ways to do this. The official number of poor people, including adults and children, in the country in 2002 was 34.6 million.[3] Dividing $522 billion by 34.6 million yields $15,087 annually for every poor adult and child. Alternatively, there are 15.3 million poor households (families and single-person households).[4] Dividing $522 billion by 15.3 million gives $34,118 per poor household.

I don't know about you, but I'd say these amounts are not small. I'd call them moderate. Using the per person measure, the country is spending enough on poverty programs to give, say, a poor family of four an income supplement of $60,348. I'd call this generous. I'd even call it enough.

Then why do some advocates of the poor say the government is not helping enough? It's because the $522 billion is not given to the poor all in cash. As noted in our list above, only $102 billion is provided in cash.

Where did the rest ($420 billion) go? Well, it goes to programs, services, and people that are, supposedly, helping the poor. These include doctors, nurses, hospitals, day-care operators, teachers, public schools, colleges, universities, farmers, and utilities. Granted, the poor get the service or help, but they don't get the cash.

Why is it this way? It's this way because taxpayers demand it. Taxpayers don't want to simply give the poor money because they're afraid the poor won't spend the money in the "right way" (booze over food!). So taxpayers have insisted on a whole host of "strings" in assistance to the poor. Taxpayers only want to help the poor if they can tell the poor what to do.

And what's wrong with this, you may indignantly ask? What's wrong with helping the poor as long as there are strings attached to the help? What's wrong is that it's an inefficient and costly way to help the poor, and many of the poor will engage in complicated behavior to get around the strings.

Let's take two examples from the medical (Medicaid) and food (Food Stamps) programs for the poor. Medicaid is the most expensive program helping the poor, and it's no wonder why. Essentially Medicaid pays for medical care needed by the poor. But because the poor aren't using their own money, they have very little incentive to worry about the cost of their medical care. This is simple economics: When something is free, it's value to the user is very low, and the service will be overused. So there are tons of stories of Medicaid patients using doctors and hospitals for treatment that others would do at home or would take steps to avoid.[5]

Don't get me wrong—I'm not bashing the poor. Anyone, poor and non-poor alike, will overuse a service if it's free. It's the economic person in us at work.

Or look at the Food Stamp Program. It's commonly known that there's been an underground Food Stamp market in low-income neighborhoods, where Food Stamps are sold for pennies on the dollar. Why? Because some poor households would prefer other things rather than food, so they're willing to sell the Food Stamps for less than their face value in order to have the cash to buy what they want.[6]

The bottom line here is that taxpayers "pay" for putting strings on the funds allocated to help the poor. The alternative is to simply give the poor cash. Cut out all the government bureaucracy and rules and regulations and simply give poor people what they value most—cash. As shown above, if all the poverty programs were converted to cash grants, each poor person or household could receive a sizable annual amount of money.

But we probably wouldn't want to give each poor person or household the same cash grant. Instead, we'd want to base the cash grants on two principles: (1) poor households who earn less would get more cash, and (2) the cash grants would decline as the poor household earned more, but they would decline at less than $1 in cash grant for every additional $1 in earnings.

The first principle ensures that those households most in need of help would get the most help. Yet the second principle is equally as important because it ensures poor households will not be penalized for self-improvement.

The second principle might work like this. Say a low-income worker earning $12,000 receives $14,000 in the cash grant, increasing total income to $26,000. Now say the low-income worker completes a training course and gets a better job paying $16,000. The cash grant would drop, but maybe only to $12,000, meaning the household's total income rises to $28,000. If the cash grant had fallen to $10,000, there would not have been an incentive for the worker to take the training course, because total income would have been the same as before the worker's increase in earnings.

The plan I've outlined above was actually proposed over forty years ago by Nobel Prize–winning economist Milton Friedman.[7] Friedman called the idea a "negative income tax" because he would have the Internal Revenue Service (IRS) operate it and simply pay the cash grants to poor households rather than collect taxes from them. Recently Columbia University economics professor Edmund Phelps proposed a similar plan based on supplementing wage rates earned by poor households.[8]

Smart Economics knows a substantial amount of money is spent each year on helping the poor. However, one problem is that little of the help is in the form of cash. Millions of nonpoor persons benefit from poverty programs by either administering them or providing services paid by the programs. Converting all poverty programs to simple cash grants would simplify our "war on poverty" while also putting money directly in the hands of the poor. But taxpayers would have to trust that the poor would know how to spend the money in their best interests.

6 Does War Help the Economy?

Whenever the country is struggling economically, you'll hear some people say, perhaps half seriously, that what the country needs is a good war. It's not that these people are warmongers. But there is a folklore that war spending can "jump-start" a stalled economy. The classic example given is World War II. Some claim it took the massive spending on World War II to bring the country out of the Great Depression of the 1930s. Some also say the increased budgets for the military during the 1980s helped the economy grow during that decade.

Certainly war spending can help certain industries and regions. Increased spending on military hardware and supplies will add to the orders and employment at firms making the products. Regions where these firms are located will likewise benefit. The economic boom in California during the 1980s was partly fueled by the military buildup and spending on advanced weapons and armaments.

However, if economics teaches us anything, it teaches us that there are both benefits and costs to any action. If the federal government spends more money for additional troops and military equipment and supplies, where do these funds come from? If they come from more taxes levied on households and businesses, then their spending will be reduced in order to increase military spending. From the point of view of the national economy, this means private spending goes down while government spending on the military goes up, so the total impact is a "wash."

Or the federal government can borrow the money to pay for the extra military spending. Yet this borrowing will come predominantly from U.S. households and businesses, so once again, money is simply transferred from private hands to government hands, and there is no net increase in spending in the economy.

Military spending implies something economists call "opportunity cost."

This simply means the money spent on the military could have been spent in some other way, such as modernizing factories or expanding educational opportunities. And the payoff from military spending and nonmilitary spending can be different, too. Spending $1 million on artillery shells to blow up targets leaves nothing in return, whereas spending that same $1 million on new factory technology can pay dividends to the business for years to come.

But before you label me as antimilitary or as a "peacenik," let me say there is an economy-wide benefit from military spending. The benefit is not to jump-start the economy or to provide jobs and income to certain people and regions. Instead, the benefit comes from the original purpose of the military—to provide *security.*

Indeed, commerce and economic opportunity and progress only flourish if people and businesses feel *secure.* That is, people and businesses won't make investments, engage in contracts and agreements, and maintain property unless they feel safe and protected. In fact, the lack of security and protection in poor, inner-city neighborhoods is one of the biggest impediments to their economic development. In this sense, police protection and public safety in the inner city is, perhaps, the most important economic development tool that could be used there.

But let's get back to our story about the military. The real benefit of the military is the protection it gives to our citizens from foreign enemies. If citizens feel protected from foreign threats, they will feel free to take risks and make long-range investments and commitments. If citizens feel threatened, they will be less outgoing, they will play it safe, and they will not be willing to think in long-run terms.

The 9/11 tragedy and its aftermath perfectly illustrate the payoff from the military. After the airliners hit the World Trade Center and the Pentagon, the national economy virtually came to a halt for several days. People's concerns naturally shifted from making money to personal survival. But as the military dealt with terrorists abroad, people gradually gained confidence and security and returned to normal commercial activity. In fact, the U.S. economy began growing and expanding again only two months after 9/11.

Smart Economics knows our economy would be better off if both the human and monetary resources spent on the military could be used in other productive capacities that expanded both our intellectual and physical accomplishments. Yet because there are apparent enemies to our peace and safety, the role of the military is to keep these enemies at bay so the rest of us can go about our daily lives without worrying about external threats.

7 Does More Spent on Education Pay Off in Student Achievement?

Right-leaning talk show hosts are fond of citing statistics like the following. In 2000, the District of Columbia (DC) spent almost $12,000 per pupil in the public schools, whereas North Dakota spent only half that amount. Yet only 7% of DC's fourth graders were considered to be proficient or advanced in math, compared to 27% of fourth graders in North Dakota.[1] Therefore, the talk show hosts conclude, spending more on public education doesn't help students.

You know that just about anything can be proven with statistics, as long as you select your statistics carefully, and the claim that spending doesn't lead to educational performance is a perfect example. I could just as easily show you that average public school spending is higher in Connecticut than in Mississippi, and students perform better in Connecticut compared to students in Mississippi. So who's right?

This is actually where *good* statistical analysis comes in handy, because most of us can't reconcile these two apparent contradictory examples with the naked eye. In fact, there are two problems with simply directly comparing spending and student performance in different states. One is that dollars don't buy the same amount of resources in each state because the cost of living does vary by state (ask anyone who's lived in both DC and North Dakota).

Also, students come to school with different backgrounds, and these backgrounds importantly affect their academic performance. Lots of research has shown that students coming from families with two parents and from families with more educated parents who earn more money tend to do better than students from single-parent families and from poorer families with parents who didn't go as far in school.[2]

When both differences in what a dollar purchases in each state and differences in the family backgrounds of students are accounted for, as

TABLE 1. Links between Student Performance, Spending, and Social Characteristics

For a 10% Increase in:	*Student Academic Achievement:*
Per Pupil Instructional Spending	Increases by 1%
The Poverty Rate	Decreases by 0.3%
Families Headed by a Single Female	Decreases by 1.1%

Source: Author's analysis of data from the National Assessment of Educational Progress.

Table 1 shows, there *is* a link between spending and student performance.[3] But the link is between spending *in the classroom* (so-called instructional spending) and student performance. Public school spending outside the classroom, on things like administration, transportation, and support services, shows no association with how much students learn. Unfortunately, nationwide almost $4 out of every $10 spent on public elementary and secondary education is *outside* the classroom.[4]

Let's get more specific. What kind of instructional spending helps students more? Is it spending on computers, other equipment, supplies, assistants to help the teacher, specialists who give students extra help in certain subjects, higher teacher salaries, or is it spending on simply hiring more teachers to lower class sizes?

Over several years I conducted an exhaustive analysis of what works best in the public schools of North Carolina. Possible links between seventeen alternative measures of student performance, eleven different school inputs, and six socioeconomic characteristics of students were examined.[5] The answer I found was (let's have the drum roll please): Hiring more teachers to lower class sizes was the school policy most frequently related to improved student test scores. This finding has been corroborated by studies in other states.[6]

This simple answer should make sense. With fewer students to teach, teachers can give more attention and help to each individual student. Also, unruly students, who harm both themselves as well as other students, are easier to control in smaller classes. This increased attention and control should lead to better learning.[7]

Unfortunately, there is one sobering message. Teachers and other school instructional inputs have limited impact. My research shows that school instructional inputs can, at most, account for 20% of the differences in student achievement.[8] The majority of what determines how well a student does in school comes from the student's family and from the student. In short, schools can only do so much.

Smart Economics has found that spending more money on schools can lead to improved student performance as long as that spending is done in the classroom. The very best thing that schools can do to help students is to lower class sizes. So smart schools will lock up the computers, quit embracing new teaching techniques, and strip administration and support services to the minimum in order to hire more teachers and reduce the number of kids in each class. If necessary, put a wall down the middle of existing classrooms to create individual spaces for the smaller classes.

Has the Social Security Surplus Been Stolen?

Although Social Security's long-run financial survival is open to question (see Chapter 9), for two decades Social Security has actually been collecting more revenues than it is paying out in benefits to retirees. In 2003, Social Security collected $138 billion more than it spent. At the end of 2004, Social Security had accumulated unspent revenues of over $1.4 billion.[1]

Of course, Social Security is collecting more than it spends now because it will need these savings, or surplus, to pay benefits to the "baby boom" retirees in the coming decades. But is there any Social Security surplus? The claim is often made, interestingly from people on both the Right and the Left, that Social Security's surplus has been "robbed" and spent by greedy politicians.

Such a claim is misleading, and here's why. No smart person lets his or her savings sit in a mattress or a safety deposit box. Doing so means the saved money doesn't earn any interest, and the savings would actually decline in purchasing power, owing to inflation. So the smart person takes savings and invests it to earn interest.

This is the case with Social Security's savings. We wouldn't want the savings sitting around, but we'd want them invested and earning interest. But the framers of Social Security in the 1930s didn't want the Social Security savings invested just anywhere. Instead, they wanted the savings invested in very safe, low-risk investments.

Ask investment experts what the safest, lowest-risk investment is, and they'll give this answer: U.S. government Treasury securities. Despite all the jokes about the federal government's management of financial affairs, the simple fact is that U.S. government Treasury securities are supersafe because the U.S. government has a perfect 200-plus-year track record of never missing an interest payment or redemption of a Treasury security. Of course, this safety is "paid for" by the relatively low interest rates earned by Treasury securities.

So the Social Security savings, or surplus, is invested in U.S. government Treasury securities. There's nothing diabolical about this, and in fact, this requirement should be applauded for maintaining the safety of the Social Security savings. How, then, can anyone claim the Social Security savings are being "robbed" and spent?

Here's how. Treasury securities are issued by the federal government when the government's revenues fall short of its spending and the government needs to borrow money. In other words, when the federal government runs a budget deficit, it borrows money by selling Treasury securities. The borrowed money is then spent.

So it is true that when the Social Security surplus is invested in U.S. government Treasury securities, the funds are then spent by the federal government. But this is the case with all investments. Money invested in stocks is spent by companies issuing the stocks. Money invested in a CD ("certificate of deposit," not "compact disc"!) is invested by the bank in a local business loan or home loan. Invested money doesn't remain idle—it does get spent somewhere.

The key questions with any investment are: (1) whether the investment will pay its promised rate of interest and (2) whether the investor will ultimately receive back his or her original money when the investment is redeemed. On both of these questions, U.S. government Treasury securities have an impeccable record. The same can't be said of stocks, corporate bonds, real estate, or any other nongovernmental investment. If the federal government failed to pay interest on any Treasury security or failed to redeem a Treasury security, the ability of the government to borrow money in the future would be severely curtailed.

Some call the Treasury securities bought with Social Security's surplus "worthless pieces of paper." This shows their misunderstanding of the investment world. If Treasury securities are "worthless pieces of paper," why do millions of investors purchase them for their private portfolios? The answer should now be obvious. The Treasury securities bought by Social Security are worthy investments that will earn interest for the Social Security surplus while providing safety for the surplus.

Smart Economics says that the hype about the Social Security surplus being robbed and replaced with worthless pieces of paper simply reveals the confusion of those making the claim about the investment world. Social Security savings are invested in supersafe U.S. government Treasury securities. In its 200-plus-year history, through good times and bad, the U.S. government has never, ever, missed paying interest on or redeeming Treasury securities. No one can perfectly predict the future, but by investing in U.S. government Treasury securities myself, I've bet this track record will continue!

9 Is Social Security Going Bankrupt?

It's a commonly accepted "fact" that Social Security, the government-run retirement fund, will be bankrupt in a few years. Polls of young people usually find they don't think Social Security will exist when they retire. Business-oriented politicians have used the belief in Social Security's ultimate demise to garner support for dramatically shifting Social Security to more of an individually based savings fund.

But like so many widely accepted "facts" about the economy, a closer examination reveals reality is much more complicated. For while Social Security certainly could go belly-up, it could also survive.

What will determine whether Social Security sinks or swims, more than anything else, is the performance of the economy. A better-performing economy will cause Social Security to last longer, while a poorer-performing economy will mean Social Security will go under sooner.

The importance of the economy in determining the future of Social Security is clearly seen in the annual report of the Trustees of the Social Security System. Each year the Trustees evaluate the financial health of Social Security and estimate how long the system will last.

The Trustees evaluate Social Security's future on the basis of three economic scenarios: a pessimistic, an average, and an optimistic economic performance. The average scenario assumes the future economy will perform roughly like its average performance over the past forty years. Under this assumption, the Social Security system will be exhausted (a polite way of saying "bankrupt") by 2041.[1] After 2042, Social Security will only be able to pay benefits to retirees at a much reduced rate.

This is the finding that receives so much press attention and is used to claim Social Security is inevitably headed toward insolvency. But note, it's one of only three scenarios examined by the Trustees.

It's shouldn't be surprising that the pessimistic scenario shows Social Security going belly-up even earlier, in 2030. But the optimistic scenario shows Social Security lasting *indefinitely*—that's right—*indefinitely*! Under this scenario, Social Security will last as far as the eye can see.[2]

Yet, you may rightly ask, isn't the optimistic scenario "pie in the sky"? Should it even be considered?

Actually, the optimistic scenario is close to the reality of the economy of the past decade. Two of the most important economic measures in the scenario are the average annual increase in worker wages, after inflation, and the average annual improvement in how efficiently businesses turn inputs into outputs—that is, business productivity. Higher values on both measures contribute to a longer life for Social Security.

The optimistic Social Security scenario assumes worker wages, after inflation, increase 1.6% annually, and business productivity improves 1.9% annually.[3] Looking at the recent ten-year period from 1994 to 2003, which includes periods of both economic growth and recession, we see worker wages, after inflation, rose an average of 1.7% annually, and business productivity increased at a rate of 2% annually.[4] So if the future economy performs at rates close to the actual performance of the past ten years, then Social Security's life will be extended by several decades.

Even if Social Security survives, some critics say it's still a bad investment for most workers. Critics say workers would be better off taking the funds they and their employer contribute to Social Security and investing on their own.

How valid is this criticism? First, we shouldn't expect the interest rate, or rate of return, earned on Social Security money to be very high because Social Security funds are legally limited to investing in ultrasafe U.S. government Treasury securities (see Chapter 8). And an ironclad rule in investing is that rates of return are lower, the greater the safety, or the lower the risk, of the investment.

There's also the fact that Social Security isn't like a typical investment, where money John Doe invests has his name on it, and John Doe's money earns interest that's credited to John Doe's account. Managers of Social Security have never made claims the system works like a typical investment.

Here's the way Social Security works. All monies paid to Social Security are put in one pot with no name labels (this is the "social" part of Social Security). The big pot of money is invested in supersafe U.S. government Treasury securities, and then a formula is used to determine how much any given person gets back from Social Security. The formula is only partly related to how much money the person paid in to Social Security. Instead, the formula works to transfer, or redistribute, some of Social Security's funds contributed by high-income workers to lower-income workers. This means Social Security is a better deal, or investment, for lower-income workers than for higher-income workers, assuming both have the same life span.

Two economists recently calculated the effective investment rates of return earned by workers of various income levels. Averaged over all workers, the economists found the effective annual rate of return to be 2.6%. However, for the poorest persons, the annual rate of return was over 4.7%, while for the richest persons it was 1.5%.[5]

Some say the ultimate solution is to privatize Social Security. This means workers take some, or maybe all, of their Social Security tax contributions and invest them in private accounts that they would direct. Rather than Social Security contributions going into one big pot with no name labels, the contributions would go into individual pots with each person's name.

In short, the privatized part of Social Security would operate like the 401K retirement plans offered by many businesses. Supporters say it would give workers a stake in their own retirement, and privatization would also increase the rate of return earned on the funds. A leftover part of Social Security would be preserved for very low income workers who don't have the financial ability to adequately save for their own retirement.

Of course, there are many, many questions to be answered and issues to be addressed about privatizing Social Security, such as what kinds of investments would be eligible, allowable risks to take, and government oversight. But one frequently overlooked question is: How would we get there from here? Theoretically, young workers could be as well off or better off with private retirement accounts. But in traditional Social Security, taxes paid today by current workers are partially used to support Social Security payments received by existing retirees and future near-term retirees. As some of these taxes are redirected to private accounts, existing and near-term retirees would be left "high and dry."

This is the *transition issue* with privatizing Social Security, and one solution is to have a temporary tax to finance the transition until everyone is under the new privatized system.[6] Depending on the degree of privatization, the tax may need to raise over $1 trillion. Unfortunately, many advocates of privatizing Social Security conveniently ignore or deemphasize this issue.[7]

Smart Economics recognizes predicting the financial future of Social Security is extremely difficult because it crucially depends on the financial future of the economy. It is not a certainty that Social Security will go bankrupt in a few decades. In fact, if the economy performs as it did in the past decade, Social Security could very well be viable at least through the rest of this century.

Also, *Smart Economics* knows Social Security doesn't operate like a typical investment in two important ways. First, it only invests in ultrasafe U.S. government Treasury securities. Second, some of the funds contributed by higher-income workers are paid to lower-income workers. Thus, Social Security is a better investment for lower-income workers.

Last, *Smart Economics* knows that turning Social Security into individual private accounts could be done, but it would involve substantial new public costs during the transition.

10 Should Our Money Be Backed by Gold?

The United States, as well as most of the industrialized world, was on a gold standard for much of its history. This meant holders of paper U.S. dollars could, if they desired, cash them in for gold. Although the vast majority of people never did this, the option of doing so gave people the feeling the paper money was backed by something real and valuable—in this case, gold.

Yet in 1933 the gold "window" was closed to U.S. citizens, and in 1971 the United States totally divorced itself from gold in international transactions. So today Americans can't legally redeem their paper dollars for gold. Some say this is the source of many of our economic problems of the past thirty years. They say a return to the gold standard would provide a stability and soundness to the U.S. economy.

One of the concerns that pro–gold standard folks (I'll call them "gold bugs") have is inflation. If there's no requirement that paper money has to be backed by a certain amount of gold, then the government is free to flood the country with paper currency. And as the old adage says, higher inflation results from "too much money chasing too few goods."

So to keep inflation in check—or saying the same thing, to keep paper dollars "strong" in their value—gold bugs want to tie the amount of paper currency in circulation to the amount of gold the government has. Sounds logical and reasonable, right?

Not so fast! One problem with a gold standard is that supplies of gold are very limited. This means it's not easy for the government to expand its holdings of gold. This further means that with a gold standard the supply of paper dollars wouldn't be expanding very much, if at all. Our supply of money would essentially be determined by countries that produce gold.[1]

And this is a problem, you say? Duh! If the supply of paper dollars is limited or fixed, won't this keep inflation low and the dollar strong, and isn't this just what is needed in the economy?

Yes, but it can also lead to another issue—deflation. Inflation is an increase in prices. Deflation is the opposite—a decrease in prices, or falling prices.

And what is wrong with falling prices? Two things, and they're both crucial to your pocketbook. At first thought you might think falling prices are great because your income will buy more. But the dirty little secret is, if all prices are dropping for an extended period, so too will your salary.

This should make sense to you. If a company's revenues are falling owing to lower prices, the company will have less money to pay its employees. So deflation in prices also can mean deflation in wages and salaries.

There's also a problem caused by deflation for people who have loans. Loans that have fixed interest rates, like many home, auto, and personal loans and credit cards, have regular payments of a specified dollar amount. For example, an auto loan or lease might require a monthly payment of $200.

Yet if deflation results in dollars becoming more valuable over time, and furthermore, if deflation results in your income falling, then deflation means the effective burden of these loan payments increases. The $200 auto loan payment becomes more burdensome if your income drops. This is the reason so many farmers and homeowners defaulted on loans during the 1930s, the last time we had extended deflation.

So if a gold standard isn't the answer, what is? First, there's more to a country's economy than its currency. What is needed from a country's money is a reliable, consistent currency that increases in availability as the economy grows. If the output of the nation's factories, farms, and offices increases 10% from last year, then the amount of dollars provided by the government should increase 10% to facilitate the additional trading and spending. Such an increase in paper dollars would not cause inflation.

The job of controlling the growth of paper dollars in circulation, as well as the growth in other forms of money like bank deposits and loans, is actually done by the Federal Reserve. Since the 1990s they've done a pretty good job because inflation has been under control during those years. So we can have a paper currency not backed by gold and low inflation if the currency is managed properly.

Smart Economics knows a gold standard isn't a cure-all for the economy. In fact, a gold standard could lead to deflation, falling salaries, and more expensive credit payments. As long as the paper money supply grows in line with the production of the economy, the dollar will maintain its value, strength, and reliability.

Should Government Enforce a Living Wage?

Millions of hardworking Americans earn very low wages. A household living on the legal minimum wage makes less than $11,000 annually. A new movement has sprung up to require businesses to pay all workers at least a "living wage."

Each supporter's definition of a living wage might be different, but generally the idea is to have businesses pay workers a wage that will be sufficient to afford an adequate, or decent, standard of living. For a family of four, this might translate to $9 or $10 an hour.

America is a compassionate society, and most of us don't like to see poor families struggling. We know that in many cases there are links between poverty and poor performance of children in school and antisocial behavior by teenagers. So requiring businesses to pay a "living" or "decent" wage to workers may seem reasonable.

Well, our compassion must confront reality. Like it or not (although if you own stocks, you'll like it), businesses operate not to employ people but to make a profit. And in the profit-driven business world, the wage paid to a worker will be directly related to the revenues the worker gains for the business.

So, if Susan Sales, a salesperson for Optimax, brings in $100,000 of sales revenues to Optimax, then Susan is worth up to $100,000 annually to the company. If Susan is good at her job and there are few others as good, Susan's salary could very well approach $100,000.

There are two problems low wage earners face. First, although what they do is important, the job just doesn't generate much revenue for the company. Second, because most low-wage jobs require few skills, many people can do the work. Both these factors translate to low wages.

Therefore, the big problem with the living wage—or its counterpart, the minimum wage—is that businesses won't keep a worker if forced to pay the worker more than he or she is worth to the business. Either the business will hire someone who does bring in more revenue, or the business will eventually replace the worker with a machine.

Economists have a reputation for disagreeing over public policy issues. However, on the issue of forcing businesses to pay workers more, numerous economic studies over decades have come to the same conclusion: Raising the minimum wage, or instituting a "living wage," increases unemployment among the affected workers, usually folks with low skills.[1] So it's not much consolation to a worker to have the government say, "Your wages are going up," and the business say, "You don't have a job!"

Does this mean we should forget about low-wage workers? No, but first recognize that the majority of those earning only the minimum wage are teenagers and the elderly.[2] Most of these workers aren't supporting a family and are working to gain experience, to earn "pocket change," or to supplement retirement pensions. Also, the majority of minimum wage workers move on to higher-paying jobs within a year.[3]

For low-wage workers who are supporting a family, there is a very important federal program that does provide additional income support. It goes by the "bureaucratese" name "earned income tax credit," or EITC. In 2003, the EITC could effectively increase a minimum wage earner's hourly earnings to almost $8 an hour. When combined with other low-income programs, such as Food Stamps, Medicaid, and child-care subsidies, the total support can move the resources of low-wage workers much closer to that needed for an "adequate" or "decent" standard of living.

Smart Economics knows businesses operate in the self-interest of their owners and stockholders. On this basis, workers are paid commensurate with what they earn for the business. Having government tell businesses what they must pay workers won't change this. If a business is forced to pay a worker more than the worker is worth to the business, then what will "give" is the worker—he or she will be canned. A better approach is to supplement low-wage workers' earnings with cash from government programs like the earned income tax credit.

12 Should Government Control the Prices of Necessities?

Whenever the price of gasoline rises, you can count on a chorus of shouts for the government to control gasoline prices. When electricity prices jumped a few years ago in California, even politicians called for price controls on electricity. When house prices or rents take a leap in some local market, you're bound to see letters to the editor in the newspaper calling for price controls on house prices or rents.

The call from consumers for price controls on products or services that they believe are too expensive is understandable. After all, each of us wants to pay the least possible for what we buy. The drumbeat for price controls is also fanned by the adversarial way the media and Hollywood portray relations between business and consumers. Through movies, TV shows, and many news stories, consumers are taught businesses make too much money and are out to cheat the buyer. Therefore, the train of thought continues, it often makes sense to restrain business by controlling the prices they charge.

What's wrong with this picture? Plenty! When businesses must compete for consumers' dollars, as is the case most of the time, the adversarial relationship is between the competing businesses, not between businesses and consumers. In this case the price charged will be pushed down to a level that is just sufficient to give businesses a "normal" profit on the amount they sell. Any attempt by a particular business to charge more will be stymied by consumers taking their buying to another competitor.

Of course, not all businesses selling the same product charge exactly the same price. Those with stores in better locations, with a better service department, or with a more helpful sales staff will be able to charge a little more. But there's still a limit to the price they can charge. If they jack up the price too much, buyers will say the "heck" with the more convenient location, better servicing, and cheerful staff—they'll go to where the price is cheaper.

In this kind of environment, price controls have some unwelcome consequences. If the price a business is charging is already the minimum necessary to cover costs and return a "normal" profit, then imposition of a law requiring the price to be lower will mean losses for the business. And businesses won't take the losses sitting down. They'll reduce the amount of the product they're willing to sell.

But buyers will react to the lower price in exactly the opposite way. A lower price will motivate buyers to want more of the product (to those of you who took Econ 101, remember the "demand curve"!).

So look at what we have as a result of price controls. Businesses will want to sell less, but consumers will want to buy more. A gap is created between buyers (demand) and sellers (supply). Or, in English, a *shortage* occurs. Yes, the price of the product is lower, but everyone who wants to buy the product at that price can't do so.

Yeah, yeah, you say, this might make sense in the ivory tower, but show me some real examples of shortages caused by price controls. Well, remember the gas lines of the 1970s? Those of you over fifty will! They were caused by domestic price controls on oil and stations running out of gasoline (a product from oil) at the legal price they could charge. Or try finding a reasonably priced apartment to rent in New York City. You can't. And what's the reason? New York City has had price controls on rents since World War II. They've resulted in much lower rates of new residential construction compared to cities of comparable size without controls.[1] The long waiting lists for surgeries in Canada are the result of that country's control of medical prices.[2] Even California's electricity brownouts in 2001 were brought on by price controls at the wholesale level of electricity production.[3]

Relatively new price control legislation has been passed in some states to prohibit what some call "price gouging" after natural disasters. If you've ever lived through a flood, tornado, or hurricane, you know that one of the outcomes is prices for items like bottled water, chain saws, tree removal services, and lumber can skyrocket. The reason is simple. These are exactly the items that people in droves want after a natural disaster. But if supplies of the items are limited, then all the new purchasing will naturally drive up the prices.

Although at the time consumers hate the price hikes and sellers are profiting from people's helplessness, actually the higher prices help the community recover from the disaster. The higher prices are like a bright light signaling to manufacturers and dealers that more money can be made by selling their wares in the disaster-ravaged region. So what do they do? Well, pronto they ship lots of new supplies of flashlights, lumber, bottled water, chain saws, etc., to the region. Within days the area is swimming in these items and, presto, prices will drop.

Government price controls will just muck up this process and delay the increase in supplies to the damaged towns and cities. Plus, the price controls will require the government to act as a policeman, making sure that prices for water and batteries don't exceed their legal limit. What a tedious job!

This brings up another downside of price controls. They require a government bureaucracy. Indeed, during the widespread price controls during World War II, thousands of new government bureaucrats were hired to make sure the controls weren't violated.

And even with the price control police force, many businesses will find inventive ways to get around the restrictions. There's the famous (at least to economists) story about plywood during the national price controls of the early 1970s. To escape the controls, manufacturers simply drilled holes in regular plywood. The holes served no useful purpose, but they did allow the manufacturers to legally claim the "holey" plywood was a "new" product not subject to the price controls on plywood. Of course, the efforts to drill the holes were wasteful from the point of view of the overall efficiency of the economy.

There is one time when price controls are a good idea. This is when they are applied to a *monopoly*—that is, to a business that totally controls the market and has no competitors. Economists can show a monopoly will charge higher prices, produce less output, and make greater profits than many competitors. In this case, price controls can reduce the monopoly's prices and profits and force it to sell more output.

In reality, monopolies are few and far between. Two common monopolies that have been regulated with price controls are electric utilities and cable TV franchises. But a far better strategy of dealing with monopolies than price controls is to simply destroy the monopoly by opening it up to competition. Allowing more than one power utility to sell electricity and more than one cable company to market cable TV in an area is the best way to lower prices and increase service.

Smart Economics says price controls are a bad idea. They're a "feel good" plan that creates shortages and frustrations among both buyers and sellers. Prices rise when buying increases relative to supply or when supplies decrease relative to buying. So to get prices to fall, either buying must be reduced or supplies must be increased. Government meddling with price controls can do neither.

13 Should Government Pay Businesses to Create Jobs?

There's a multimillion-dollar bidding war going on in the country, and it's using your money. No, it's not taking place in Las Vegas or the nearest riverboat gambling casino. It's actually being done by elected politicians, and to top it off, it's all perfectly legal.

Calm down—the politicians aren't playing roulette or five-card stud with your tax money. But they are betting—betting they can entice businesses to come to their state or community.

The betting is called "business incentives," and they've become pervasive across the country. Here's how they work. State or local government bureaucrats, usually working through commerce or economic development departments, recruit a business to come to the area. The business will be told about all the great things in the area, like schools, workforce, and climate. But the icing on the cake may often be money (a.k.a., incentives). The money can come in many forms—a cash grant, forgiveness of taxes, or building of roads or sewers to serve the business.

Why's this done? Why are government officials giving money to businesses to come to their town or state? Shouldn't it work the other way? Shouldn't businesses be paying taxes and other fees, just like households do, for the privilege of locating in a community?

Government officials say they have no choice. In order to attract businesses with their jobs and payroll to a community, government officials say they often have to provide these monetary incentives. If not, the business will just go to some other place that pays "incentives."

In fact, the incentives game can become a vicious bidding war. State A offers Fido Company $20 million worth of incentives to locate in A. Then State B offers $30 million. State A comes back with a $35 million counteroffer, and so on. Fido Company just sits back and eagerly watches the ante keep rising. In fact, in 1993 an intense bidding war between several southeastern states ultimately resulted in Alabama offering the former Mercedes Benz Auto Company an incentives package worth as much as $500 million.

Clearly incentives are popular among businesses establishing a new location, but are they popular among all businesses? Well, let's say Fido Company takes the $35 million incentives package and locates in State A. But suppose Dogpatch Company, a competitor to Fido, has been in State A for years and is a homegrown company that never received incentives. Will Dogpatch be happy with Fido getting $35 million in taxpayer money? Of course not. In fact, Dogpatch will resent the money given to Fido. In effect, some of Dogpatch's money paid in taxes is being used to subsidize the competing company, Fido.

Let's get to the bottom line. Do business incentives work; that is, do business incentives really attract new jobs and income? On one level, the answer is no. Surveys of business executives commonly find incentives are at the bottom of the list of factors considered in locating a company. Labor force availability, worker quality and cost, access to roads and airports, quality of schools, cost of living, climate, and taxes and government regulations are the key characteristics executives say they compare in deciding where to locate their operations.[1] Incentives are hardly on the radar screen!

But other studies find business incentives can be important. A study from the National Bureau of Economic Research painstakingly compared communities that won a new firm using incentives to runner-up communities—the community that was almost picked by the firm.[2] The study found winning communities had significantly greater job and income growth as a result of landing the new firm than did runner-up locales.

Confused? On the one hand, business executives say incentives aren't important, but on the other hand, communities that use them seem to do better economically. Can these two findings be reconciled?

Yes, they can. Businesses appear to use a two-step procedure in deciding where to locate a new facility. First, they screen locations based on all the factors executives say are important—labor, climate, costs, taxes, etc. This results in two or three communities as finalists for the facility, and these communities are similar in all the important factors.

The second step is to choose between the finalists. This is where incentives are important and where incentives can actually be the deciding factor.

Unfortunately, this doesn't leave public decision making in an easy place.

They can spend limited public money on education, worker training, and roads, or they can reduce taxes in order to get on the list of finalists for new factories and facilities. Or they can spend public money on incentives to be the winner among the finalists.

Most states have decided to do both. And although business incentives are a political hot potato, a very small share of state and local government spending is actually allocated to them.[3]

So states and localities seem to be behaving reasonably. The overwhelming majority of their public money is spent on factors businesses say are vitally important in their location decisions. A very small fraction is spent providing the extra nudge of incentives.

When business incentives are considered, states and localities need to put them in a cost/benefit framework. Don't blindly give businesses cash to come. Instead, estimate the economic benefits, in terms of new income, jobs, and taxes, from a new business location, and compare these to the economic cost of the incentives. Where there's a big net plus, the incentives can be justified.

Smart Economics realizes business incentives are a controversial economic tool that many say are unfair and unneeded. Yet research shows they can be crucial in winning a new business, and they can pay off when compared to the new income, jobs, and tax revenues created by the new firm and its offshoots. The key is to put business incentives in a cost/benefit framework and use them where the expected benefits exceed their costs.

14 Can Government Create Prosperity?

When something goes wrong in life, we often look to government to fix it. Probably nowhere is this more the case than with the economy. When the economy isn't performing well—for example, when the economy is in a recession—people across the political spectrum, from the Right to the Left, call for action by the government.

What can the government, and particularly the federal government, do to right the economic ship if it has run aground? Those on the right side of the political spectrum immediately say, "Lower taxes." The theory is, if taxes are lowered and more money is put in the hands of businesses and consumers, they will spend these additional funds and stimulate the economy back to recovery.

Folks from the left side of the political table also recommend financial action from the federal government, but their recommendation often is different. The Left wants the government to spend more money on things like roads, bridges, and schools. The Left's idea is that if businesses and consumers aren't spending money during a recession because they're pessimistic about the economy, then government can pick up the slack. Government spending on infrastructure will create jobs and income and, more important, increase optimism in the economy so businesses and consumers will also begin to spend.

Although the "cut taxes" versus "increase government spending" recommendations seem like polar opposites, they really have a similar economic problem that is their Achilles' heel: Where does the money come from for the tax cuts or the added government spending?

The federal government can get its money in two ways: tax it away from businesses and households, or borrow it from businesses and households. Simple logic indicates that if the government cuts taxes without reducing spending, or if it increases spending while leaving taxes unchanged, then it must increase its borrowing.

And where does the borrowing come from? It comes from the same businesses and households who would get the tax cuts or benefit from the increased government spending (some borrowing could come from for-eigners, but only about $2 out of every $10 borrowed).[1] So in terms of the impact on the whole economy, the tax cuts or increased government spending would be virtually a net wash when the required borrowing is considered.

Let me be clear—there are some cases where tax cuts or added gov-ernment spending could help the economy. If the tax cuts were *combined* with reductions in *wasteful* government spending, or if the new spending on vital government functions was combined with an elimination of other wasteful government spending, then the economy could be improved by these actions. But, unfortunately, usually this isn't what is done!

There is another avenue by which the government can supposedly en-sure prosperity, and this is by actions from the group of superbankers known as the Federal Reserve (or Fed). Without boring you with details, suffice it to say the Fed acts as the central bank, or banker's bank, of the United States. Most countries have an institution like our Fed. And among the Fed's considerable powers is the ability to move interest rates on short-term loans up and down.

So when the economy hits a speed bump and slips into a recession, the usual call, from both the Right and the Left in unison, is for the Fed to reduce interest rates. Lower interest rates are supposed to motivate busi-nesses and households to borrow and spend more, and this will cause pros-perity to return.

Now, a little voice in your head might be saying that this sounds too simple. Well, your little voice is correct. It is too simple, and a closer look shows flaws in the interest rate prescription.

To see why, you have to know one other piece of information. To change interest rates, the Fed has to manipulate the amount of paper money and moneylike forms, such as bank deposits, in the economy. Think of the in-terest rate as the price of money. So just like the price of apples falls if more apples become available, the interest rate falls if the Fed creates more dollars (and conversely, the interest rate rises if the Fed slows the creation of money).

Therefore, interest rates do drop if the Fed suddenly bumps up the cre-ation of paper dollars. But there may be a surprising and undesirable con-sequence. The new dollars will be absorbed into the economy in one of two ways. The "good" way is if they're absorbed by spending on *additional* products and services from the nation's factories, farms, and offices. This would mean prosperity has returned because economic production has increased.

But the "bad" way is if the extra dollars are simply absorbed by higher prices, that is, by higher inflation. This means prosperity hasn't returned. And to make matters worse, it means interest rates will go back up, because there's a virtual one-to-one correspondence between the level of interest rates and the level of the inflation rate.[2]

So the Fed can only create prosperity if its policy of reducing interest rates by increasing the supply of money results in factories, farms, and offices immediately upping their output to absorb the new dollars. But there's no assurance this will happen. If it doesn't, then the increased money will result in higher inflation, and interest rates will go back up to where they were—or maybe higher.

Government tax and spending policy can have one limited effect on prosperity: on its timing. These policies may not change the total spending of consumers and businesses, but they can change *when* the spending occurs. So tax cuts, increased government spending, and Fed interest rate cuts can cause more spending today at the expense of less spending tomorrow, when the adverse effects of the policies come home to roost. But sometimes there just may be an election in between!

Smart Economics says the government can't create prosperity through its manipulation of taxes, spending, and interest rates. Real prosperity is ultimately created by individuals and businesses working hard, creating new inventions and innovations, and delivering a final product that is valued by buyers. The government does serve a role by helping to create an environment in which prosperity can flourish. This includes instituting a simple and sensible tax and regulatory system, ensuring safety, spending money on the vital functions of government, and allowing people to reap the rewards of their sweat and toil.

 Economic Questions
about How Much Taxes
Are Paid, Who Pays Taxes,
and the Fairness of Taxes

15 Do We Pay 60% to 80% of Our Income in Taxes?

The numbers sound scary: Americans pay somewhere between 60% and 80% of income in taxes. No wonder so many households are poor and others live paycheck to paycheck. The government is taking all our money!

You've heard such numbers parroted by various radio talk show hosts and others. But how accurate are they? If you don't like paying taxes, you may *want* to believe the percentages because they provide an easy excuse for why your standard of living isn't as high as you'd like.

Well, I have to burst your bubble again. It's simply "flat not true" that the tax burden is between 60% and 80%. If we take all the federal, state, and local taxes collected by government and divide by all the income earned in the country, the tax burden in 2003 was 27%.[1] Furthermore, although this percentage has edged up in recent decades, the jump hasn't been that significant. For example, in 1959 government at all levels taxed away 24% of income in the country.[2]

Of course, what I'm quoting here is the *average* tax burden, based on comparing total taxes collected to total income generated in the country. Different percentages can be derived when different comparisons are made.

For example, a think tank called the Tax Foundation periodically calculates the direct and *indirect* taxes combined paid by the average American family. Direct taxes include obvious taxes like income, sales, and Social Security taxes. Indirect taxes include those that are directly paid by businesses but, the Tax Foundation assumes, are passed on to families in the form of higher product prices.

The Tax Foundation's numbers show a higher tax burden than cited above. In 1998, the tax burden was put at 39% for the average two-earner family and 38% for the average one-earner family. Also, these burdens were more than twice as high as the burdens in the mid-1950s.[3]

Not all economists would agree with the Tax Foundation's methods for calculating the tax burden. How much of business taxes are "passed on" to families in the form of higher prices is a rather complicated process to analyze, and assuming all these taxes are ultimately paid by families may not be appropriate. Nevertheless, even if we accept the Tax Foundation's methods, the average family's tax burden is just shy of 40%, not 60% to 80%.

Of course, all the numbers presented thus far are "averages," and as is often stated, no one is average. There are big differences in the tax burden of families and households, especially when income is considered.

Specifically, the tax burden tends to *rise* with the taxpayer's income. The percentage of income directly paid in taxes (not including business taxes) by households is over four times higher for the richest households compared to the poorest households (Figure 4).[4] Much of this difference is due to the fact that the federal income tax is a *progressive tax*, which results in higher levels of income being taxed at higher rates (see Chapter 16). In 2002, the richest 1% of taxpayers paid 24% of their income in federal income taxes, compared to the poorest 20% of taxpayers who not only paid no federal income taxes but effectively *received* a payment from the IRS equal to 4% of their income.[5]

If the claims that Americans pay 60% to 80% of their income in taxes

FIGURE 4. Tax Burden Rises with Income

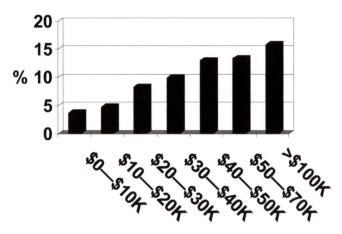

Source: U.S. Bureau of Labor Statistics, *Consumer Expenditure Survey, 2002.*

is bogus, why do such claims get started and spread? There are three possible explanations.

One is exaggeration. Remember the tale of John telling his friend about a 5-pound fish he caught. By the time the story worked its way through ten other people, John had caught a 100-pound fish! The same can be true of the tax burden. The burden is continually inched higher as more people talk about it.

A second reason is confusion between the *average* tax rate, or burden, and the *marginal* tax rate. While on average Americans pay between 30% and 40%, depending on the calculation, of their income in taxes, they can pay much higher rates on additional, or marginal, income.

For example, let's track the taxes paid on $1,000 of additional income to taxpayer Joe Smook. Let's say Joe is in the highest federal income tax bracket of 35%. This means Joe pays 35% of any additional income he earns to taxes (more on tax brackets in Chapter 16). Let's also say his state has an income tax, and his state income tax bracket is 7%. So right out of the gate, Joe loses $420 of the $1,000 to state and local income taxes for a *marginal* tax rate of 42%.

But it can get worse. If Joe spends the remaining $580 and his state has a 7% sales tax, this is another $41 in sales taxes, so now the total tax payment is $461 ($420 + $41). Or if Joe invests the $580 and it becomes part of his estate passed on to his heirs, as much as a third could be taxed away by the federal estate tax. This would amount to $191 (⅓ of $580). In this case, the total tax on the $1,000 would be $611 ($420 + $191). Thus, a lifetime marginal tax rate of between 46% and 61% would be levied on Joe Smook's additional $1,000 of income.

Last, there are some *projections* made by serious economists that the average tax burden *could* reach as high as 60% to 80% in the future. Professor Laurence Kotlikoff wrote an interesting book titled *Generational Accounting* in which he calculates that such a lofty tax burden may ultimately be needed in order to fund Social Security, Medicare, and similar commitments made by the federal government.[6] Of course, whether such a tax burden would occur is pure speculation (I doubt the American public would stand for it). Thankfully, this tax burden doesn't exist now.

Smart Economics recognizes claims that the average tax burden is between 60% and 80% are pure exaggeration. The current true average tax burden is most likely 30% and at most 40%. However, the total tax rate paid on *additional* income can be much higher, perhaps as high as 60%. Also, there are predictions that the average tax burden could be much higher in the future unless dramatic changes are made to large federal programs like Social Security and Medicare.

16 Does a Tax Bracket of 40% Mean the Government Takes 40% of Your Income?

Even people who aren't tax experts have heard of the term *tax bracket*. The problem is, they've heard about it but don't really know what it means. And ignorance can lead to misunderstanding and misuse.

When most people hear a phrase like, "John Doe is in the 40% tax bracket," they assume it means John Doe pays 40% of his income in taxes. This is just flat wrong!

There are two major reasons why the statement isn't correct. First, people pay income taxes on their *taxable* income, not their *gross* income, or earnings. There are several items used to reduce gross income to taxable income, including personal exemptions and deductions. For example, in 2005, a four-person family with gross income of $60,000 would pay federal income taxes *not* on $60,000 but on $37,200, over one-third less than $60,000.[1]

Second, people pay *different* tax rates on different parts of their taxable income. Table 2 shows the federal income tax rates paid by a married couple on different ranges of taxable income in 2005.[2]

So let's say the Tyler family has gross income of $169,900 and taxable income of $147,100. They pay a federal income tax rate of 10% on the first $14,600, 15% on the next $44,800 ($59,400 − $14,600), 25% on the next $60,550 ($119,950 − $59,400), and 28% on the remaining $27,150 of taxable income ($147,100 − $119,950).

It can correctly be said that the Tylers are in the 28% federal income tax bracket, since their taxable income of $147,100 falls in the taxable income range where 28% applies. But this means they pay 28% on additional taxable income, *not* that they pay 28% of all their income in federal income taxes. In fact, Table 3 shows the Tylers pay 18% of their *gross* income in federal income taxes.

So a tax *bracket* refers to the tax rate paid on additional taxable income.

TABLE 2. Federal Income Tax Brackets for Married Couples, 2004

Taxable Income Range	Tax Rate
$0–$14,600	10%
$14,601–$59,400	15%
$59,401–$119,950	25%
$119,951–$182,800	28%
$182,801–$326,450	33%
Over $326,456	35%

Source: Research Institute of America, *Federal Income Tax Handbook, 2005*, section 1103.

TABLE 3. Calculation of the Tyler Family's Federal Income Tax

Status: Two adults and two children

Gross Income: $169,900

Taxable income after personal exemptions and standard deduction: $147,100

Tax calculation:

$14,600 × 0.10	=	$1,460.00
$44,800 × 0.15	=	$6,720.00
$60,550 × 0.25	=	$15,137.50
$27,150 × 0.28	=	$7,602.00
Total tax owed:		$30,919.50
As % of Gross Income:		18%

It also goes by the name *marginal tax rate.* A tax bracket does *not* measure the percentage of gross income paid in taxes. Instead, this concept is measured by another term, the *average tax rate.* In the case of the Tylers, their average tax rate for federal income taxes is 18%, whereas their tax bracket is 28%. For the federal income tax, the average tax rate and tax bracket aren't the same because the federal income tax is a *progressive* tax system, meaning a higher tax rate is paid on higher ranges of taxable income (again, see Table 2).

Of course, there are taxes other than the federal income tax, and each of them has its own rules and complications. But the same rule applies: The average tax rate is the percentage of gross income paid in taxes, while the tax bracket, or marginal tax rate, is the tax paid on an additional dollar of taxable income. For some taxes, like the sales tax in most states and the FICA (Federal Insurance Contributions Act, which funds Social Security and Medicare) tax for most households, the two tax rate measures will be the same.[3]

Now that you have the idea of tax bracket under your belt, there's another "smart economics" use for it. How often have you heard someone refer to a specific expenditure as a "tax write-off"? What is implied is that the tax write-off is good because it reduces taxes owed. And what is further implied, or assumed, is that the write-off reduces taxes $1 for every $1 in the write-off. So if some big-shot businessperson spends $3,000 on a trip to Vail but can claim it as a "business tax write-off," then the trip costs the big shot nothing!

Well, think again. If a businessperson believed this, he or she wouldn't be in business very long. This is because tax write-offs that are classified as *tax deductions,* which are most of them, *don't* reduce taxes dollar for dollar with the write-off. Instead, every dollar of a tax deduction will reduce your taxes by an amount equal to your *tax bracket.* So if the business big shot who went to Vail is in the 33% federal tax bracket, and if the $3,000 expense is a legitimate business tax deduction, then the big shot's federal income taxes are reduced by $990 ($3,000 × 0.33). That's still a saving, but it also means the big shot pays for the majority of the Vail trip.

The same calculation applies to the biggest consumer tax write-off, interest paid on a home mortgage. If the Tylers spent $8,000 on mortgage interest, their tax savings is not $8,000 but $2,240 ($8,000 × 0.28).

Are there some tax write-offs that reduce taxes dollar for dollar with the write-off? Yes, they're called *tax credits.* There are many fewer tax credits than there are tax deductions, but if you're lucky enough to qualify for one, they can really lower your tax bill. The most common tax credits are the earned income tax credit for low-income working taxpayers, a tax credit for families with children, and a tax credit for families that pay for child care. However, there are "bells and whistles" on qualifying for them.

Smart Economics distinguishes between tax bracket and average tax rate. Particularly for the federal income tax, your tax bracket *doesn't* measure the percentage of your income paid in taxes. Also, *Smart Economics* recognizes that "tax write-offs" called deductions *don't* reduce your taxes dollar for dollar with the write-off. For most taxpayers, every dollar of a tax write-off will reduce federal income taxes by less than 30 cents.

17 Can Cutting Tax Rates Increase Tax Revenues?

When tax cuts are debated, one side has an easy answer, one that my mother would have called a "have your cake and eat it too" position. They say cutting tax rates won't reduce tax revenues to the government, because tax revenues actually *increase* when tax rates are *reduced*.

The tax cutters' reasoning is that lower tax rates will stimulate people to work more and businesses to produce more because both will keep more of what they make with a lower tax burden. So tax cuts cause the economy to grow bigger, and a bigger economy will mean more taxes are paid to the government.

Although this logic does have some valid points, there is one fatal flaw—the math doesn't *necessarily* work out. Even if the economy expands when tax rates are cut, there's no necessity the economy will expand enough to counteract the effect of the lower tax rate. For example, suppose average federal income tax rates are cut from 30% to 25%, and this causes taxable income to increase from $6 trillion to $6.5 trillion. Income tax revenues will still fall from $1.8 trillion (0.30 × $6 trillion) to $1.6 trillion (0.25 × $6.5 trillion).

Also there's the problem of disentangling the effects of a tax cut from the effects of normal economic growth. With very few exceptions, the economy continually grows, which means taxable income and tax revenues are constantly rising. So tax revenues can go up after a tax cut simply as a result of regular growth in the economy unrelated to the tax cut.

To see this, look at Figure 5. Tax revenues increase over time both when there is no tax cut and with a tax cut. Supporters of tax cuts can say, "See, tax revenues rose after tax rates were cut." While true, what the tax cutters miss is that tax revenues would have increased even more with no tax cut. In Figure 5, while tax revenues rose from $1 trillion in the first year to $1.2 trillion in the fourth year with the tax cut, tax revenues would have risen to over $1.3 trillion in year four without the tax cut.

FIGURE 5. A Tax Cut That Loses Revenue

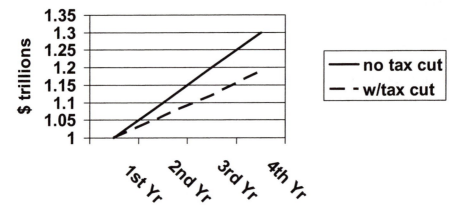

The difference between the solid line and dashed line in Figure 5 can be used as the "cost" of a tax cut. The cost of a tax cut is the tax revenue that could have been collected, but isn't, when tax rates are cut. Serious studies of tax cuts measure the losses of tax cuts this way.[1]

Can any tax cut go against the math discussed above and result in tax revenues growing faster than they would have without the cut? That is, can the lines in Figure 5 be reversed, with the upper line applying to cutting the tax rate?

Yes, when the tax rate being cut starts from a very high level. Very high tax rates deter people from working and businesses from operating. Why work, for example, if the government takes 70% or 80% of what you earn? So cutting tax rates from such lofty and confiscatory levels can unleash so much economic activity that tax revenues could be higher with the tax cut than without it.

Where is the "break point," above which reductions in tax rates gain tax revenue for the government but below which a tax rate cut does result in tax losses? Most studies agree that certainly tax rates above 75% are above the break point, and for some taxes, the break point is around 50%.[2] So for tax rates above 75% and perhaps above 50%, a tax rate cut stands a good chance of generating more taxes to the government.

It's important to realize these tax rates are combined for all levels of government. So, for example, if the federal government's income tax rate is 40% and your state's tax on income is 20%, the combined tax rate is 60%.[3]

In this case, cutting either the federal or state income tax rate could increase tax revenues.[4]

Fortunately, most tax rates today are below 50%. This means tax rate cuts generally lose tax revenues for the government. Does this mean I'm against tax cuts? Certainly not! Actually, I think the American tax burden is too high on many households. But for those of you who support this view, let's not overdo the argument by claiming too much. Let's not claim tax cuts can more than "pay for themselves" when they don't, just to garner support for the cut.

Smart Economics says that most tax cuts lose tax revenues for the government. Tax cuts may appear to "pay for themselves" because the economy is usually growing each year, unrelated to the level of taxes. However, cuts from tax rates that are extremely high, for instance, above 75% and perhaps above 50%, can "pay for themselves" by causing the economy to grow much more rapidly.

18 Will a Tax Cut of $1 Create $7 to $10 of New Income?

An often-made claim made by supporters of tax cuts is that every dollar of a tax cut will multiply, ripple, or turn over so many times in the economy that, when all is said and done, each dollar of the tax cut will have created $7 to $10 of additional income.

But I'm really being unfair to single out tax cutters as being behind this claim, because other groups are, too. Supporters of government public works projects, such as spending on roads, bridges, and public buildings, often state the same claim. Likewise, some private sector groups also get into the act. Private groups who support spending on museums, sports facilities, or parks often predict big payoffs to the spending.

Like most simplistic economic statements, there's a grain of truth in the assertion that a tax cut of a dollar will create more than a dollar of income. Dollars spent in the economy do ripple through economic sectors and change hands many times. If $1 million is spent building a bridge, much of that money will be spent paying workers. In turn, the workers spend the money on groceries, gas, clothes, rent, etc., meaning the money becomes income to the grocer, gas station operator, shop owners and workers, and others. And again, the grocer, gas station operator, and shop owners and workers will spend the money on products and services they buy, which means the money becomes income to even more people.

So, then, why isn't it true that a dollar in tax cuts can grow to be several more dollars of income? Well, for one, because much of the dollar will be lost each time it changes hands. Taxes will take some of the money, as will savings and, importantly, spending on products and services that are made outside of the local economy or the nation. For example, most of the money spent on a new car at an auto dealership in your hometown will go outside of the town to wherever the car is made.

Economists have actually spent a good deal of time calculating what the "multiplier" is for spending. When these "leakage" effects are accounted for, most multipliers are in the 1.5 to 2.5 range, rather than 7 to 10.[1] Thus, a tax cut of $1,000 will ultimately result in $1,500 to $2,500 of new income. Likewise, new spending on a public project of $1,000 will mean additional income of $1,500 to $2,500.

Some of you may be thinking, "OK, so the multiplier is only 1.5 to 2.5 rather than 7 to 10; it's still bigger than 1." Well, not so fast! The multiplier works both ways. If government spending is reduced by $1 million in order to have a tax cut of $1 million, there's a negative multiplier associated with the reduced government spending and a positive multiplier with the tax cut. The two multipliers can easily cancel each other.

Or if taxes are increased by $1 million in order to allow the government to spend another $1 million, there's a negative multiplier connected to the tax hike and a positive multiplier with the spending increase—and, again, the two may cancel.

But what if the government cuts taxes but doesn't reduce spending, as the federal government frequently does? Won't this leave us with only a positive multiplier?

Although this may seem like a "gotcha," it's not. This is because the government will have to borrow money from private sources to make up the difference, and so there will be a negative multiplier associated with less money spent by private individuals and companies who make the loans (for more on this, see Chapter 14).

Does this mean we can ignore these multiplier effects? No, we can't for three reasons. First, there are multiplier effects associated with *private sector* spending, and communities may want to know the size of these impacts. For example, if a new manufacturing plant comes to town with a $10 million annual payroll, using the multiplier will tell local residents that the total annual economic impact of the plant will likely be between $15 million and $25 million.

Second, when the government changes taxes and spending, it's not always the case that the two are both changed in the same locality. Taxes may be increased in one region or state in order to fund public projects in another region or state. In this case, both localities, the one paying and the one receiving, may want to use the multiplier to calculate the total impact of the tax hike or the public spending. Of course, the total impact will be negative in the community paying more taxes and will be positive in the community receiving the public project.

Last, although multiplier effects may cancel each other, they don't always. Multipliers can be of different sizes within the 1.5 to 2.5 range. So if a 1.5 multiplier is attached to a government spending reduction of $1 million, but a multiplier of 2 is associated with the corresponding tax cut of $1 million, then the total impact on the economy will be positive.

Smart Economics says that "multipliers" associated with changes in taxes or spending are *not* in the 7 to 10 range. Instead, they are in the 1.5 to 2.5 range. Further, multipliers must be applied to both sides of the equation. For example, if government spending is reduced in order to give a tax cut, then a multiplier must be applied to both the spending reduction and the additional income provided by the tax cut. Or if taxes are increased to increase government spending, then the positive effect from the spending will essentially be canceled by the negative effect from the tax hike.

19 Do Corporations Pay Too Little in Taxes?

Need some more tax revenue for the government? Some politicians have an easy answer—just tax corporations. After all, these politicians say, corporations and their CEOs (chief executive officers) are rich. Corporations make plenty of profits and CEOs earn big salaries, so paying a little more in taxes won't hurt them.

Plus, the share of taxes paid by corporations has been falling. In 2003, corporations paid 7% of all federal taxes. A decade earlier, the share was 10%, and in 1960 corporations paid 23% of federal taxes.[1]

Unfortunately, this is probably the prevailing view among most people. I say "unfortunately" not because I'm necessarily a fan of corporations but because people are being deceived by the politicians calling for more corporate taxes. The fact is, those who ultimately pay corporate taxes are not the people you may think.

But before I get to that, what exactly is a "corporation"? Well, a corporation is *not* a person, but it is a form of business organization. Owners of the corporation (shareholders) pool their money and hire a manager (CEO). The CEO then hires the workers, purchases or rents the equipment, factory, and other inputs, and implements a plan for producing and selling a product or service to customers. And after all costs are paid—salaries to the CEO and other workers, payments for all the inputs, etc.—hopefully there's money left over (profits) that's paid to the shareholders.

This very brief description of a corporation reveals three important facts. First, shareholders of the corporation own it. The CEO is an employee (albeit a high-paid one) just like the factory workers. Second, the corporation is simply an organization through which money passes. So taxing the corporation is just a way of taxing the money that goes in and out of this organization. Third, the "players" involved with the corporation—shareholders, workers including the CEO, and customers—are candidates for paying any taxes levied on the corporation.

Now let's see what happens when the government puts a tax on a corporation. Initially, the corporation will likely have no choice but to pay the tax out of profits. So the immediate effect (economists call this the "short-run" effect) of a corporate tax is reduced profits for shareholders. (And before you say shareholders are all rich people, don't forget that the mutual fund you own probably has investments in corporations!)

But after initially taking lower profits to pay the tax, won't shareholders then instruct the corporate CEO to increase the prices charged to customers? They may, and if they do, buyers of the corporation's product or service will end up paying for some of the tax. While certainly some of these buyers will be rich, even more will be middle class or poor. Thus, rather than rich CEOs and shareholders paying the corporate tax, many average- or lower-income households will effectively pay *part* of the tax bill.

Notice I said *part* of the tax bill. That's because corporations likely won't be able to pass on the entire tax bill to customers in the form of higher prices. Consumers aren't just passive pawns in the economic game. Corporations know consumers always balk at paying higher prices. Corporations know consumers will buy less at higher prices, or they will shift their purchases to other sellers (single-owner or partnership companies and foreign firms) not affected by the corporate income tax. Both these actions will prevent corporations from jacking up the price by the full amount of the tax.

The rest of the tax will come out of the corporation's "hide," so to speak. Some will come from lower profits, some from less investment in equipment, buildings, and technology, and some from lower salaries to the CEO and other workers.

Does this mean a tax on corporations is a sham? Actually, yes! Corporations can't pay taxes because a corporation is not a separate economic entity. A corporation is just a legal creation. The substantive parts of the corporation are the owners, workers, and customers. It's these people who will pay a corporate tax. The only question is the share that each pays. Research shows that ultimately the majority of the corporate income tax is effectively paid by shareholders and workers.[2]

Hence, a corporate tax just hides the ultimate tax on corporate shareholders, corporate workers, and corporate customers. Indeed, this may be why some politicians like corporate taxes—because the effective impacts of the tax are hidden. An *honest* tax policy would scrap corporate taxes and explicitly tax stockholders, workers, and consumers. But who said all tax policy was honest!

Smart Economics recognizes that corporations don't pay taxes because they can't. Corporations exist only in the legal world. In the economic world, corporations are combinations of investors (shareholders) and workers who sell something to customers. It's these three groups—shareholders, workers, and customers—who bear the burden of a corporate tax. The only question is how much each group pays.

20 Would Rich Investors Benefit from a Flat Tax?

There are several proposals around to change the way the federal government collects taxes. One of these proposals is an idea called the *flat tax*. The flat tax would make two major changes to the federal income tax code. First, it would eliminate the six tax brackets (see Chapter 16) and replace them with one rate (hence the term "flat" rate). Second, it would eliminate all tax exemptions, deductions, and credits and replace them with one large household deduction based on number of people in the household.[1]

The flat tax would be a major overhaul of the federal income tax, and as such, it has sparked much debate and controversy. Among the many criticisms of the flat tax is that it's a gift to the rich. The flat tax on individuals would only tax wages, salaries, and pension benefits. Investment income earned by individuals, such as dividends and interest, wouldn't be taxed. Because dividend and interest income tends to be higher for higher-income persons, it's claimed the rich would "make out like a bandit" with a flat tax by having major parts of their income go untaxed.

We can deal with this claim rather quickly. It's not true! In truth, what the flat tax would do is tax dividend and interest income *once* instead of *twice* as under the current income tax system.

Yes, you read my statement correctly. Today, dividend and interest income are taxed twice, once at the corporate level where the dividends and interest income are generated and then at the individual level when the dividends and interest are paid to households. This double taxation of dividends and interest has long been noted by economists and cited as a deterrent to saving and investing.[2]

The flat tax would end this double whammy of taxation by taxing dividends and interest only once. The flat tax could tax dividends and interest either at the corporate level or at the individual level. It really doesn't matter because individual investors in corporations are the owners of the corporations.

Framers of the flat tax choose to tax dividends and interest at the corporate level for a simple reason: Taxing income closest to the source of its generation is easiest and more likely to include all the income. As income moves away from its source, there's more opportunity for some of it to be lost or diverted.

So taxing corporate dividends and income instead of taxing those monies when they are paid to individual investors is really favorable to those who want all income taxed. Unless, of course, those people want some income taxed more than once!

Smart Economics knows that double taxation of dividends and interest is not only unfair; it also discourages saving and investing. The flat income tax would end this double taxation by taxing dividends and interest only once—at the corporate level.

21 Is the Sales Tax Regressive?

Taxes come in three varieties: regressive, proportional, and progressive. Although some may want to attach the label "good" to progressive and "bad" to regressive, I want you to approach these tax topics with an open mind.

The federal income tax is the best example of a progressive tax. A progressive tax is a tax where the *percentage* of a taxpayer's income paid in taxes is higher for higher-income taxpayers than for lower-income taxpayers. The federal income tax is progressive because federal income tax rates are higher for higher levels of taxable income (see Table 2 in Chapter 16).

A proportional tax—some call it a "flat" tax—is a tax where the percentage of a taxpayer's income paid in taxes is the same for taxpayers of all incomes. So, for example, a proportional tax of 10% means all taxpayers pay 10% of their income in the tax.

Now what about the regressive tax? A regressive tax is a tax where the percentage of a taxpayer's income paid in the tax is *lower* for higher-income taxpayers than for lower-income taxpayers. For example, a tax is regressive if high-income taxpayers pay 5% of their income in the tax, but low-income taxpayers pay 10% of their income in the tax.

However, it's important to recognize a regressive tax doesn't necessarily mean higher-income taxpayers pay less money for the tax—they just pay a smaller *percentage* of their income in the tax. If Bill Bigbucks earns $100,000 and pays 5% in a particular tax, that equals $5,000. But Lou Lowmoney earns only $20,000, and if he pays 10% of his income for the same tax, his tax bill is $2,000. So although Bill Bigbucks pays a lower percentage of his income for the tax, he does pay more money.

So how can regressive taxes occur? Are there some taxes that specifically charge low-income taxpayers a higher tax rate and charge high-income taxpayers a lower tax rate?

No, this doesn't happen. The most commonly claimed regressive tax is the *sales* tax, and the supposed regressivity occurs like this: Let's say the sales tax is 5%. Let's go back to Bill Bigbucks, with an income of $100,000, and Lou Lowmoney, whose income is $20,000.

Now if Bill and Lou both *spent* all of their income and paid a 5% sales tax on this spending, then the sales tax would be a *proportional* tax because both taxpayers would be paying 5% of their income in the sales tax.

But what if Bill Bigbucks invests $20,000 of his income and spends $80,000, while Lou Lowmoney spends all of his $20,000? Then Bill pays the 5% sales tax on $80,000, for a tax bill of $4,000, while Lou again pays the 5% sales tax on his $20,000. But while Lou's sales tax bill is still 5% of his income, Bill's is lower. Notice that for Bill his $4,000 sales tax bill is 4% of his $100,000 income. So, based on these numbers, the sales tax is regressive.

Indeed, this is the traditional view of the sales tax. Since all taxpayers pay the same sales tax rate and since higher-income taxpayers spend a smaller portion of their income than do lower-income taxpayers, higher-income taxpayers end up paying a *lower percentage of their income* for the sales tax. This is precisely why many groups oppose the sales tax and oppose replacement of the federal income tax with a federal sales tax.

But is the traditional view correct? I claim it's not, and here's why. Comparisons like those between Bill Bigbucks and Lou Lowmoney are only a snapshot at a single point in time. Yet most households don't plan their lives for a single year but instead plan over several years. For instance, the $20,000 that Bill Bigbucks saves today may be used in five years for the purchase of a new car. Therefore, although Bill doesn't pay sales tax on the $20,000 today, he will pay sales tax on the money in five years when it is spent.

What this means is that we shouldn't claim the sales tax is regressive just by looking at one year of spending. Instead, we must look at spending over the *lifetime* of taxpayers.

And guess what? When the lifetime spending of households is examined, it is found that households of all income levels pay roughly the same percentage of their income for the sales tax.[1] In other words, the sales tax is a *proportional tax*, not a regressive tax. Furthermore, if the poor do pay a higher percentage of their income in sales taxes than the rich, it is because the poor tend to spend more of their money on products that have higher sales taxes applied, like cigarettes, alcohol, and gasoline.[2] So whenever politicians increase taxes on the so-called sins (cigarettes and alcohol) and gasoline, the poor are hit harder than the rich.

Smart Economics judges whether a tax is regressive by looking at lifetime spending rather than spending in a single year. When this is done, the sales tax is found to be roughly proportional, not regressive. If lower-income households do pay a higher percentage of their income in sales taxes, it's because they tend to spend a greater percentage of their income on high-taxed products, like cigarettes, alcohol, and gasoline.

22

Do the Rich Get a Break on Social Security Taxes?

How's this for a tax system: Earn $20,000 and pay 6.2% in taxes; earn $50,000 and pay 6.2% in taxes; earn $90,000 and pay 6.2% in taxes; but on any money you earn *over* $90,000, you pay no *additional* taxes.

If this seems like a weird tax system, I agree. But it's a tax system that virtually all of us know, because it's the Social Security tax system.

That's right, I said the Social Security tax system. The Social Security tax is really very simple. You pay a 6.2% tax rate on any income earned from working up to $90,000. But you pay nothing on any labor income over $90,000.[1]

Just so you're clear on this: If Dagwood earns $40,000, he pays $40,000 × 0.062, or $2,480, in Social Security tax. But if Blondie earns $100,000, she pays $90,000 × 0.062, or $5,580, in Social Security tax but pays nothing on her remaining $10,000 ($100,000 − $90,000).

Seems unfair, right? If you agree, you have plenty of company. There have been numerous proposals to extend the 6.2% tax to every dollar of a person's labor income. Supporters say this would end the "regressive" nature of the Social Security tax—meaning, people earning more than $90,000 effectively pay a lower Social Security tax on their total earnings than people making less—and it would also give Social Security more funds to help its financial solvency.

But rather than being fair, extending the Social Security tax to all income would be just the opposite: unfair!

This is because there's a very simple reason for the Social Security tax structure. Workers earning more than $90,000 don't pay additional Social Security tax on those extra dollars because what they eventually get back from Social Security doesn't increase beyond that received at the $90,000 level.

Retirees who earned more while working generally receive back more in Social Security benefits. But this only happens up to a point. And that point, in 2005, was $90,000. So taxing workers' earnings beyond $90,000 would require them to pay more taxes with nothing in return. I would call this unfair.

In fact, even with its current tax system, Social Security is already stacked in favor of workers earning less money. This is because the formula used by Social Security to calculate monthly benefits to retirees replaces a higher percentage of lower earnings than of higher earnings.

For example, in 2005, Social Security replaced 90% of a worker's first $592 of monthly earnings, 32% of monthly earnings between $592 and $3,567, and 15% of monthly earnings over $3,567.[2] Consequently, the percentage of a retiree's preretirement income replaced by Social Security declines as the income rises (Figure 6).

Rather than being a reverse Robin Hood system (robbing from the poor to give to the rich), it looks like Social Security is behaving like the original Robin Hood—but maybe with "contributing" replacing "robbing"!

Smart Economics knows why the Social Security tax stops at a certain income level ($90,000 in 2005). It's because this is where the maximum amount of retiree benefits is reached. Increasing the tax rate beyond this income level without paying more benefits would be taxation with no compensating return.

FIGURE 6. Social Security Replaces Less for Higher-Income Retirees

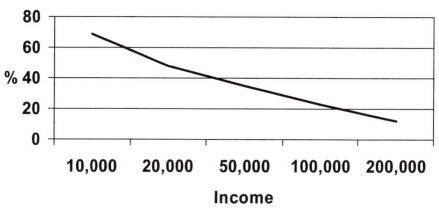

Source: Author's calculations from Social Security Administration data.

23 Has the Tax Penalty for Marriage Been Ended?

What? Why would there be a tax penalty for being married? Well, according to Congress's chief fiscal watchdog, the Congressional Budget Office (CBO), there may have been a penalty in the past for being married. The CBO estimated that in 1996 over 21 million married couples paid an average of almost $1,400 in additional federal income taxes due to being married rather than remaining single. The total "marriage tax penalty" totaled $29 billion.[1]

Exactly what does this mean? What it means is that 21 million married couples would have paid $29 billion *less* in federal income taxes if they paid taxes as single persons. The mere act of getting married, with no change in their total income, resulted in their federal income tax bill going up.

But wait; there's more. Did you know that in 1996 another 25 million married couples paid a total of $33 billion *less* in federal income taxes as a result of being married rather than single. These couples found their federal income tax bill *decreased* by an average of $1,300 because of being married.[2] That is, they received a *tax bonus* from being married.

But wait: Hasn't there been something in the news about Congress and the president "fixing" the marriage penalty? And if so, have the marriage tax bonuses also been ended?

Before answering these questions, let's see what couples used to get a tax break and which paid a tax penalty for being married, and why. In general, married couples with one earner or with one earner making substantially more money than the other earner typically paid less federal income taxes as a result of marriage. In contrast, married couples with two earners making about the same amount of money often paid more federal income taxes compared to being single.

But why? It all has to do with the complexity of the federal income tax code. A big source of marriage tax penalties is the progressive nature of the federal income tax (see Chapter 16). Built into the federal income tax is the idea that higher-income dollars are taxed at higher rates than lower-income dollars. This is based on the notion, which is silly to some, that richer households should pay income taxes at a higher rate because those households have a greater ability to do so.

What this means is that when two single people, each earning about the same income, get married, their incomes are stacked one on top of the other, and more of that total income is taxed at a higher rate compared to if the two people remained single. This was less of a problem for a married couple, one of whom earns much more income than the other.

Another source of the problem was the "standard deduction." This is an amount of money that all taxpayers can take to reduce their taxable income. Although the standard deduction is bigger for married couples than for single taxpayers, it was traditionally *not* twice as big for marrieds versus singles.

Again, this hurt married couples where each person earned about the same income. Since the married standard deduction was not twice as big as the single standard deduction, when the two people got married, they effectively had a reduction in their standard deduction. This made the taxable income of the married couple higher than the combined taxable income of the two people if they had remained single.

Yet this didn't hurt, and may actually have helped, married couples where one person earned the bulk of the family income. For example, if Joe, who earned $60,000, married Sue, who earned nothing, then Joe and Sue's tax bill would have been lower as a result of marriage because they benefited from the higher married standard deduction.

But let's get back to the original question of this chapter: Has the marriage penalty, especially, been ended?

Well, there's good news, and there's bad news. In 2003 and 2004, Congress and the president did effectively end the marriage penalty for some married couples by doubling the size of the standard deduction for married couples compared to singles and by doubling the size of the income range for the lower tax rates (the 10% and 15% rates) for marrieds compared to singles. But some marriage penalty still exists for higher-income married couples because the upper income tax brackets (those higher than 15%) weren't expanded.

Furthermore—and here's the really bad news—these changes were made temporary and are set to expire in 2009.

There is a very simple way to end all the confusion over marriage tax penalties and bonuses. This is to have the federal income tax changed to apply to *individuals* rather than to households. That is, have each individual file income taxes and make the tax paid be irrespective of marital status. Then there would be no tax consequence of marriage. This was actually the standard for federal income taxes prior to 1948.

A second simple solution is to make the standard deduction for married couples twice that for single persons *and* to eliminate the progressive nature of the federal income tax. That is, tax all dollars at the same rate. Here households could still pay federal income taxes, but marriage would not have an impact on the amount.

Smart Economics recognizes that even if the recent changes to the federal income tax code are extended, all tax penalties related to marriage have not been eliminated. The best way to take marriage out of the federal income tax code is to tax individuals instead of households or to implement a simple *flat* (or one-rate) federal income tax.

Economic Questions about What Business Does and Why and How That Affects Jobs, Consumers, and the Country

24 Is American Manufacturing Dying?

Employment in manufacturing in the United States peaked in 1979 at 19 million workers. In 2003, manufacturing employment nationwide had fallen to 14.7 million. Manufacturing employment as a percentage of total employment was a mere 11.3% in 2003.[1]

Many say this is proof positive that manufacturing is on the decline in our country. They say that soon U.S. consumers will be buying all their manufactured products from overseas companies, and all U.S. factories will be shut down.

But what if I told you that the output from U.S. factories has almost *doubled* since 1980 or that, since the mid-1950s, U.S. manufacturing output has jumped over 400%? You might say, "No way."

Well, "Way!" These statistics are absolutely correct. At the same time that employment in manufacturing has been falling, factories have been churning out more manufactured products. In fact, except during recessions, U.S. manufacturing output tends to increase each year (Figure 7).

Of course, I'm talking about manufacturing production in total. Certainly, not all manufacturing sectors have changed at the same rate, and some have actually declined. For example, from 1980 to 2003, manufacturing of computers and electronic products increased 2,500%, motor vehicles and parts increased 160%, and chemical products rose 61%. In contrast, over the same time period iron and steel production fell 15%, and clothing manufacturers reduced their production by 40%.[2]

"How can this be?" you might ask. "How can manufacturing production *increase* while manufacturing employment has *decreased*?"

You probably can answer this question if you think about it long enough (or for other readers, it may be on the tips of your tongues). The answer is one word: *productivity*. Today's manufacturing workers are teamed with much better equipment and technology than their counterparts years ago.

FIGURE 7. U.S. Manufacturing Output Has Been Increasing

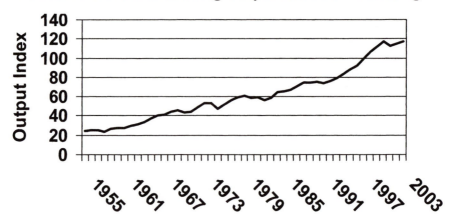

Source: U.S. Department of Commerce, Bureau of Economic Analysis,
http://www.bea.doc.gov; Federal Reserve System, http://www.federalreserve.gov.

This means each manufacturing worker can run rings around his or her predecessors in terms of output produced per hour. One measure of productivity (output per hour of work) of manufacturing workers shows it increasing 145% from 1980 to 2003.[3] So fewer manufacturing workers are needed to produce more manufactured output compared to years ago.

In fact, what has been occurring in manufacturing is similar to what's occurred in agriculture over a longer time period. After World War II, over 10 million people worked in agriculture in the United States. Today, that number is down to under 3 million.[4] Yet over the same period, farm output has increased 150%.[5] As a result of using modern machinery, technology, and planting techniques, each farmer today produces eight times more than his counterpart did after World War II.[6]

It's also important to realize that the trends of falling manufacturing employment but rising manufacturing output are worldwide. South Korea, Russia, the United Kingdom, China, Japan, and Brazil have all had bigger percentage declines in manufacturing employment in recent years than the United States.[7]

Are these trends good or bad? I think they're good. The workers who have been released from manufacturing and agriculture have provided the labor for expansion in areas like the professions, health care, education, and the tech sector. And as Chapter 25 shows, the new jobs created in our economy recently have paid more than the manufacturing jobs that have been lost.

It's likely we'll continue to see fewer and fewer people employed in manufacturing at the same time factories are producing more, just like on the farm. Further, the future workers in manufacturing will be more highly skilled and trained in the latest technology and production methods. And this means, they'll be paid more!

Smart Economics knows to measure the importance of manufacturing by how much is produced, not by how many people work in manufacturing. Gauged by production, the picture is very clear. U.S. factories have been producing more, not less. Only during recessions do factories make less, and this is temporary. Better technology, equipment, and know-how are substituting for raw brawn and muscles to keep the factory floors humming.

25 Are Low-Paying Jobs Replacing High-Paying Ones?

During the thirteen-year period from 1990 to 2003, almost 4 million jobs in manufacturing firms were lost, whereas 23 million jobs were gained in nonmanufacturing companies.[1] I've talked to hundreds of blue-collar, office, and executive audiences alike, and the common perception is that the country has been losing high-paying manufacturing jobs while gaining low-paying service jobs.

In beginning to persuade you why this perception is wrong, first you need to know that the important determinant of what individuals are paid is not the *industries* they work in but what *occupations* they have. There are tens of thousands of high-paid managers and scientists working in service companies, just like there are thousands of lower-paid laborers working in factories.

Second, you must realize that the "service" sector is a gigantic, very diverse set of industries and occupations. Essentially the service sector is all industries outside of manufacturing, agriculture, mining, and construction. The service industry therefore includes janitors, fast-food restaurant workers, and supermarket cashiers, but it also is composed of lawyers, doctors, chemists, nurses, and teachers. The range of pay for service workers goes from $10,000 to well above $100,000.

So the best way to proceed is to examine changes in *occupational jobs* over time. The important question is, Are we replacing high-paying *occupations* with low-paying *occupations* in our economy?

This is easily answered by looking at changes in jobs by occupation over a long enough time period to represent a trend. Here I look at occupational job changes over the period 1990 to 2001.[2]

Table 4 shows the eight occupational categories that gained jobs and the three that lost jobs. You can see that while the salaries of the occupational losers were all in the $20,000 range, the salary range for the occupational gainers went from $16,000 to $55,000. Big job gains were in low-paying occupations (restaurant workers) but were also in middle-paying occupations (teachers) and high-paying occupations (professional, managerial, and technical workers).

The assertion that we've been trading high-paying jobs for low-paying jobs is not correct! The average salary of the occupational gainers was $31,751, compared to a salary of $26,824 for the occupational losers. This is why, despite the large loss of blue-collar manufacturing jobs, per person earnings in the United States increased 15% from 1990 to 2001, even after taking out inflation.[3]

Yet the picture about occupational change is not entirely rosy. Among the occupational gainers, two-thirds of the jobs paid a salary above that of

TABLE 4. Changes in Nonfarm Occupations, 1990–2001

Occupations Gaining	Number Gained	Salary
Construction	2,239,430	$35,450
Restaurants	2,212,660	$16,720
Teachers	1,971,480	$39,130
Professional, Managerial, Technical	1,564,730	$55,077
Health-Care Support	1,150,870	$21,900
Administrative Support and Clerical	847,590	$27,230
Cleaning Services	840,340	$20,380
Protective Services	691,990	$32,530
Total	11,519,090	
Weighted Average Salary		$31,751
Occupations Losing	Number Lost	Salary
"Blue-Collar"*	1,365,770	$26,560
Marketing and Sales	669,760	$28,920
Personal Care Services	171,950	$21,010
Total	2,206,770	
Weighted Average Salary		$26,824

*Includes occupations in factory production, transportation and material moving, and installation, maintenance, and repair.

Source: Author's calculations using data from the U.S. Bureau of Labor Statistics, http://www.bls.gov.

the occupational losers. But this still means one-third of the new jobs paid a salary less than that of the occupational losers. Specifically, these included jobs in health-care support, cleaning services, and restaurants. And the factor separating the higher-paying jobs from the lower-paying ones will continue to be education.

Will the future repeat the past? If forecasters from the federal government's Department of Labor are to be believed, the answer is yes. Over the 2002–2012 decade, the biggest job gains will be in the professional, management, technical, and related fields on the high-pay side, adding about 9 million jobs, as well as in the restaurant, health-care support, and clerical fields on the low-pay side, with over 5 million new jobs.[4]

So there will be plenty of higher-paying jobs for the taking. But to get them, a person must have formal education beyond high school, usually a four-year college degree. And herein lies the dilemma. First, just as in the past, many people simply aren't "cut out" for going to college. But unlike years ago, increasingly these folks won't be able to take a factory job and earn a good living. My father was a high school dropout, yet he was able to earn a decent living from 1945 to 1990. Now most of the jobs available for high school dropouts, or high school graduates for that matter, will be lower-paying restaurant, general retail, and health-care assistant occupations.

Second, as job downsizing in our factories likely continues, forty- and fifty-year-old displaced factory workers won't be able to move to an equal- or better-paying job unless they're willing to spend some time upgrading their skills and education. And, quite simply, most of them won't have the time, money, or inclination to do this. So in our increasingly competitive, worldwide economy, the message is one I'm sure you've heard before: To get a good job, you must get an education.

Smart Economics realizes the economy is ever changing, and with it changes in occupations occur. In recent years there's been a movement away from factory and "blue-collar" jobs to "white-collar" and service jobs. However, two-thirds of the new jobs pay more than the lost factory jobs, and the fastest-growing occupations have been professional and managerial jobs. But to get the high-paying, "new economy" jobs, education is the key.

26 Are Companies Outsourcing Good-Paying Jobs?

In late 2003 it was reported that tech giant IBM planned to shift over 4,000 programming jobs to foreign countries.[1] While the report also indicated IBM expected to increase total employment in North America, some commentators said the movement of good-paying programming jobs to overseas locations represented an important new development. Now, not only could lower-paying manufacturing jobs be sent to foreign countries, but also professional and technical jobs requiring a college education could be shipped out of the United States. Are no jobs safe?

Yet take a trip through states like Ohio, Tennessee, Alabama, and South Carolina, and what do you see? Among other things, you see auto manufacturing plants owned by foreign companies. These companies have built the plants and established jobs here, in the United States.

The point is that both outsourcing (U.S. jobs going to foreign countries) and insourcing (foreign companies putting jobs in the United States) occur on a regular basis in our economy. U.S. companies may find it useful to establish operations in a foreign country, either to take advantage of lower costs or to be closer to the country's consumers. Similarly, foreign companies may want a production or sales force in the United States to be close to U.S. buyers or to utilize America's high-skilled labor.

Unfortunately, there are no official definitions of outsourcing and insourcing. Should all jobs U.S. companies put in foreign countries be considered outsourcing, including retail jobs in fast-food restaurants? What about contracting? If a U.S. business cuts positions here and then contracts with a foreign company for that work, is this also outsourcing?

The lack of generally accepted definitions means estimates of outsourcing and insourcing vary. One economist calculated 215,000 business, professional, and technical service jobs were outsourced from the United States from 2000 to 2003.[2] But another study argued outsourcing helps the U.S.

economy by making companies more efficient and profitable. The study suggested that two U.S. jobs were created for every job outsourced.[3]

Both these studies are based on judgments and estimates and not head counts. There is an actual government head count we can use that relies on defining outsourcing as all jobs of U.S. companies in foreign countries and insourcing as all jobs of foreign companies in the United States. Although everyone won't agree with these definitions, they do allow a look at actual numbers and trends, and so I'll use them here.

As with everything in economics, outsourcing and insourcing must be put in perspective. As a percentage of total U.S. jobs, the latest numbers (from 2001) show outsourced jobs stand at 7% (9.8 million outsourced jobs compared to 132 million total U.S. jobs). Insourced jobs in 2001 are 4.8% of total U.S. jobs. And the gap between the number of outsourced and insourced jobs has actually narrowed over the past quarter of a century, from 6.1 million jobs in 1977 to 3.4 million jobs in 2001 (Figure 8).[4]

In what industries are these outsourced jobs, and how do they compare to jobs established here by foreign companies? Table 5 gives the answer.

There were about one-third more outsourced jobs than insourced jobs in 2001. A higher percentage of outsourced jobs were in machinery and "house goods" machinery, and a much bigger percentage of insourced jobs were in other services.

But let's look at what's happened to outsourcing and insourcing since

FIGURE 8. Gap between Outsourcing and Insourcing Narrows (millions of jobs)

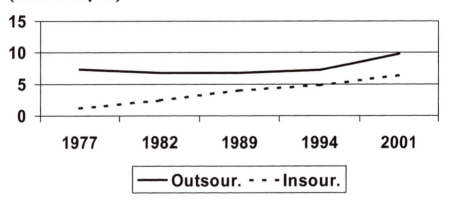

Source: U.S. Department of Commerce, Bureau of Economic Analysis, http://www.bea.doc.gov.

TABLE 5. Outsourced Jobs and Insourced Jobs Existing in 2001

Industry	Outsourced	Insourced
Total #	9,775,600	6,371,900
Manufacturing		
Machinery (%)	25.2%	18.1%
"House Goods" (%)	12.7%	6.5%
Other (%)	13.3%	15.2%
Services		
Professional (%)	17.0%	14.4%
Other (%)	28.4%	42.7%
Agriculture, Resources, and Construction	3.4%	3.1%

Machinery manufacturing: machinery, computers, electronics, transportation equip.
"House goods" manufacturing: food, clothing, wood and furniture products, paper and printing.
Other manufacturing: chemicals, plastics and rubber, nonmetallic minerals, primary and fabricated metal, miscellaneous manufacturing.
Professional services: professional, technical, scientific, and financial services.
Other services: wholesale and retail trade; transportation, management, and clerical services; health-care, lodging, and food services; miscellaneous services.

Source: U.S. Department of Commerce, Bureau of Economic Analysis, 2004, http://www.bea.doc.gov.

two major free trade pacts—the North American Free Trade Agreement (NAFTA) and the WTO (World Trade Organization)—were agreed to in 1994. From 1994 to 2001 U.S. companies increased their foreign employment by 2.5 million jobs. Over the same period, foreign companies increased their employment in the United States by 1.5 million jobs. In percentage terms, this was about the same rate of increase.[5]

But the composition of outsourcing and insourcing was much different. Look at Figure 9. Jobs are divided into five categories: machinery manufacturing (including vehicles, computers, and electronics), "house goods" manufacturing (textiles, apparel, and wood and paper products), other manufacturing (chemicals and metals), professional services (professional, technical, scientific, and financial services), and other services (wholesale and retail trade, management, clerical, lodging, and food service).

Outsourcing exceeded insourcing except in one category, machinery

FIGURE 9. Changes in Job Outsourcing and Insourcing, 1994–2001 (thousands)

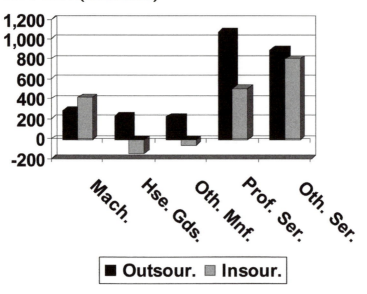

Source: U.S. Department of Commerce, Bureau of Economic Analysis, http://www.bea.doc.gov.

manufacturing. During 1994–2001, foreign companies sent 50% *more* machinery manufacturing jobs to the United States than U.S. companies sent to foreign countries. And these jobs paid very well, averaging $65,000 in salaries and benefits.[6]

Also notice the outsourcing of professional and technical jobs, like computer programmers, is not new. Over 1 million professional service jobs were sent to foreign countries by U.S. companies during the seven-year period.

(1) So what does all this mean? (2) Should we worry about job outsourcing? (3) Is it a crisis? (4) Could your job or my job be the next sent overseas?

Here are the short answers to questions 2, 3, and 4: yes, no, and maybe! Job outsourcing is a part of our economy, but its importance has been overblown by the headlines. At most, job outsourcing accounts for less than 10% of U.S. jobs, and when the job insourcing by foreign companies is accounted for, the net loss of U.S. jobs is currently only 2.6%.[7]

Furthermore, the heavy machinery manufacturing sector of the U.S.

economy has actually gained more jobs from insourcing than it has lost to outsourcing in recent years. The United States is still the world leader in technical and equipment manufacturing, and foreign companies have recognized this advantage by moving jobs here.

The jobs that are candidates for outsourcing are those that can be performed routinely and that don't require a high degree of personal interaction. Although twenty years ago computer programming was new and "cutting edge," today many programming tasks are straightforward and common and, relatively speaking, don't require a high degree of skill. These are the kinds of technical jobs that can go to foreign countries with lower costs.

So the message for U.S. computer programmers is this: Go beyond entry-level programming, which is now commonplace, and arm yourself with more specialized and advantaged computer skills. Make yourself more valuable, more unique, and therefore not interchangeable with the millions of programmers worldwide.

Smart Economics recognizes job outsourcing is not new, and it is partially counterbalanced by foreign companies putting businesses and jobs in the United States. Indeed, since the NAFTA and WTO trade agreements were established, the United States has actually gained more jobs from the *insourcing* by foreign companies than it's lost from outsourcing in the manufacturing of machinery, electronics, and equipment. Also, the gap between the number of outsourced and insourced jobs has narrowed in the last twenty-five years.

A worker can gain some protection against outsourcing by acquiring more skills and working on projects that require a large amount of personal interaction and communication.

27 Will Free Trade Destroy Our Economy?

Free trade is perhaps the most polarizing economic issue in America today. On one side are people who say free trade will be the death of the U.S. economy—or at least the death of the prosperous U.S. economy. This group thinks free trade is slowly moving all good-paying jobs to other countries, and ultimately all American workers will be hamburger flippers, cashiers, and janitors.

On the other side are free trade advocates who claim trade helps our economy by opening up foreign markets to U.S. companies and allowing U.S. consumers to buy lower-priced products. These folks say increased world trade over the last fifty years is greatly responsible for the general rise in prosperity.

I'll argue that reality lies *in between* these two extremes. Free trade pacts and agreements, like NAFTA and the WTO, result in a change in the "rules of the economic game" that creates sets of winners and losers. Among the winners are the workers of companies that can now export more and consumers who can buy cheaper foreign imports. But losers include workers in companies that lose sales to foreign imports. And while the losing workers may eventually recover, it can take decades for them to do so.

Table 6 shows NAFTA and the WTO gave free traders one thing they wanted: more trade. Both U.S. exports and imports increased dramatically after the 1994 signing of NAFTA and the WTO. Most categories of exports increased twice as fast as overall growth of the U.S. economy, and imports increased even more.[1]

Yet because imports increased more than exports after NAFTA and the WTO, it can be argued that the U.S. trade deficit increased as a result of NAFTA and the WTO. Indeed, the increase in the annual average trade deficit in Table 6 comes to $182 billion. However, not all of this increased deficit can necessarily be attributed to the trade agreements. During the

TABLE 6. Average Annual Change in U.S. Exports and Imports in Years after NAFTA and the WTO*

Category	Exports	Imports	Change in Trade Balance**
Agriculture & Food	+33.7%	+60.0%	−$3.2 billion
Industrial Supplies	+56.6%	+80.7%	−$46.6 billion
Capital Goods (except autos)	+89.6%	+123.0%	−$10.4 billion
Autos and Parts	+75.3%	+79.2%	−$40.0 billion
Consumer Goods (except autos)	+86.3%	+110.4%	−$83.0 billion
Other Goods	+20.9%	+25.3%	−$1.8 billion
Services	+50.0%	+70.1%	+$3.0 billion

*Comparing annual averages in the quantity of exports and imports for the eight years from 1995 to 2002 to the eight years from 1987 to 1994; all dollars are in 2002 purchasing power values.
**Minus (−) for increase in deficit; plus (+) for decrease in deficit.

Source: Author's calculations from data from the U.S. Department of Commerce.

1990s, the U.S. economy grew 14% faster than the economies of the rest of the world, which means U.S. purchases of products from other countries would increase more than sales of U.S. products to those countries.[2] Therefore, the extra trade deficit of $182 billion is adjusted downward by 14% to $156 billion.

What about the effects of this increased trade deficit on jobs and salaries? Using average relationships between production, salaries and wages, and jobs, I estimate the additional annual average trade deficit of $156 billion has resulted in a *loss of 1.4 million jobs and $98 billion in lost wages and salaries!*[3]

This sounds pretty bad and is certainly consistent with the doom predicted by anti–free trade groups. But it's not the end of the story.

First, the dollars "lost" through trade deficits do return to the United States in the form of foreign investments (for more discussion of this point, see Chapter 29). And these investments create jobs and income in the United States. So this logic suggests NAFTA and the WTO have resulted in the United States trading away some jobs and salaries for other jobs and salaries.

Second, and perhaps more important, NAFTA and the WTO have allowed American households and businesses access to lower-priced foreign-made products. If these products fit the needs of U.S. consumers, it means U.S. buyers can save money and use the savings to purchase other things in the U.S. economy, which also creates jobs and incomes.

This is the whole idea of trade. John Doe specializes in what he does best, and Sally Smith does the same. They trade, making each better off. It's the same with countries. Economists have a fancy term for this idea—*comparative advantage*. Just like people, if countries specialize in what they do best and then trade, their standards of living will rise.

Look at Figure 10. It shows price trends in selected consumer products where imports have increased significantly since NAFTA and the WTO. There is a clear break in the trends at 1994, the year when NAFTA and the WTO were signed. Up until 1994, the prices of all three consumer goods were rising along with the overall price level. But since 1994 overall prices have continued to rise, but prices for apparel, toys, and furniture have fallen. In 2003 U.S. consumers saved $42 billion from buying lower-priced clothes, toys, and furniture, compared to what they would have paid if the price trends prior to 1994 had continued.[4]

Of course, this is only part of the savings from trade because the United States imports more than just clothes, toys, and furniture. From 1995 to 2002, average import prices fell, while domestic U.S. prices rose. As a result, U.S. buyers of imports saved an annual average of $140 billion dur-

FIGURE 10. Prices Fell after Trade Deals (1984 = 100)

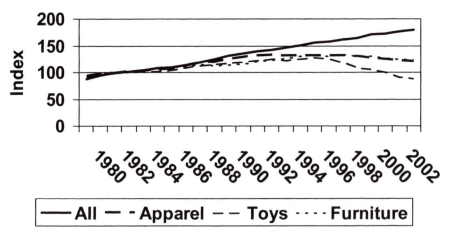

ing this time period and $293 billion in 2002.[5] These amounts actually underestimate the savings from imports because they don't include any initial price savings from imports existing in 1994.

So the bottom line in all these numeric gyrations is that a case can be made that the benefits from the freer trade since 1994 have exceeded the costs. Certainly some industries and workers have suffered, but both business and household buyers have benefited, and foreign investment in our country has increased.

But there's a rub. The losers from free trade are not the same as the winners, *and* the winners have not compensated the losers. Although there are programs to help workers displaced by trade agreements, they are little more than Band-Aids.[6] There's no serious effort to use some of the gains from free trade to help those hurt by the trade deals.

What would a serious effort look like? Here's an example. Hundreds of thousands of U.S. textile and apparel jobs have been cut after trade barriers were reduced following NAFTA and the WTO. Yet U.S. buyers of clothing are saving about $20 billion annually by being able to now purchase lower-priced foreign-made apparel products.[7]

A 5% special retail tax on all clothing bought by U.S. consumers would raise $10 billion annually. This is enough to pay every former textile and apparel worker fired since 1994 a total of $12,000 *every* year.[8] The ex-workers could use the money to pay bills, retrain, or move to a region with better job prospects.

And notice what this program would do. It would seriously assist workers who have lost their jobs through no fault of their own. But it would still leave half of the gains from free trade in the hands of consumers. So the "winners" would compensate the "losers" and still have money left over.

Smart Economics recognizes that free trade agreements are not all bad or all good; instead, they're a combination of bad and good. That is, free trade agreements benefit some segments of our population while hurting other segments. When cost savings to consumers and added foreign investment are considered, it appears NAFTA and the WTO have helped more than hurt the U.S. economy. But what has been lacking is a concerted plan to use some of the gains from trade to assist those workers who have lost their jobs.

28 Can U.S. Workers Compete with Low-Paid Foreign Workers?

The differences are amazing. The average American manufacturing worker earns over $20 an hour. The average Mexican manufacturing worker gets the equivalent of only $2 per hour, and factory workers in the country of Sri Lanka earn just money corresponding to $3 a *day* for an eight-hour workday.[1]

How, then, can American factory workers compete with their Mexican and Sri Lankan counterparts? Isn't it simply a matter of time before all manufacturing jobs, and other jobs for that matter, leave the United States for foreign countries?

Before you answer yes and begin making plans for a subsistence living, consider this. What if an American factory worker, who earns ten times more in an hour than a foreign worker, can produce twelve times more output in that hour than the foreign counterpart? Which worker would a company prefer to hire?

Hopefully the answer is clear—the American worker. What matters to a business is not what a worker is paid in isolation but what the worker is paid in comparison to what that worker can produce. So a worker who is paid ten times more but manufactures twelve times more product is actually *cheaper* to a business than the alternative, lower-paid worker.

But aren't all workers essentially alike worldwide? How can a worker in one country produce twelve times more than a worker in another country?

Easy! The worker can be better trained, can be paired with better machinery, and can know how to use advanced technology. And infrastructure is important. Workers are more productive if they work in regions with better roads and modern transportation facilities. This both allows supplies to move to factories easier and permits final products to be shipped faster to buyers.

Finally, don't forget the economic system. Studies find that workers in countries with an open, competitive economic system are more productive than those with centrally, bureaucratically controlled economies.[2]

When the cost of labor necessary to produce a unit of output is compared across countries, the United States looks very competitive, even with its high labor costs. In 2002, this cost, called *unit labor costs* by economists, was 8% lower for U.S. factories compared to the average factory in twelve major manufacturing countries.[3]

The reason for the United States's good showing is the high productivity (translated: output per hour) of U.S. factory workers. Overall, U.S. workers are well trained and highly skilled and are matched with the most modern equipment and technology. They also operate in one of the most open and competitive economic systems in the world.

I know what you're thinking. If U.S. factory workers are really low cost when their productivity is considered, why are manufacturing jobs dropping like flies?

There are two reasons. First, as discussed in Chapter 24, manufacturing jobs are falling worldwide. Millions of workers in every manufacturing country are being replaced with high-tech machines and know-how. So just as we don't need as many farmers today to grow more food than ever before, not as many factory workers are required because each worker is responsible for producing much more than his or her earlier colleagues.

Second, the U.S. edge in unit labor costs doesn't extend to every industry. In some sectors, like clothing manufacturing, countries with large surpluses of low-cost labor and primitive technology can still outcompete countries with high-skilled (and high-cost) labor and modern technology. This is why so many U.S. textile and apparel jobs have been lost once the trade barriers on foreign-produced clothing were lowered.

Before closing this chapter, let me bring up a related issue. Go back to the Sri Lankan factory worker earning the equivalent of $3 a day. Americans will read this and shudder, because we'll rightly ask how anyone could live on $3 a day!

Well, few could live on $3 a day in the United States. But Sri Lanka is not the United States. Wages are much lower in Sri Lanka, but so too are prices. Earnings similar to $3 a day in Sri Lanka will buy much, much, much, much more than $3 spent daily in the United States. This is not to deny that Sri Lanka is a poor country—it is—but the point is that earnings must always be judged by what the money can purchase in a locality.

That's why someone earning $100,000 in most rural areas can live like royalty compared to someone earning $100,000 in New York City.

Smart Economics knows businesses gauge labor costs *not* by how much a worker is paid but by how much a worker is paid compared to how much the worker produces. By this measure, U.S. manufacturing workers are still very competitive with manufacturing workers in other countries, particularly in high-tech and machinery industries.

29 Do Countries Prosper Only If They Run a Trade Surplus?

To help understand the economy, many people create analogies between national economic situations and personal finance. Most families know if they continually spend more than they earn, they'll ultimately face financial trouble.

Some like to make the same statement for the nation with respect to trade with foreign countries. So if the United States continually buys more products and services from other countries than it sells to those countries—this is called a "trade deficit"—won't this eventually mean monetary trouble for our country? Just like a person running up large credit card debts, doesn't a trade deficit mean the country is living beyond its collective means?

If you think a trade deficit could be a problem, you have plenty to worry about recently. For over twenty years, the United States has annually imported more products and services from other countries than it exported to those countries. In 2003, this trade deficit was almost $500 billion.[1]

Of course, $500 billion is a very large number to any individual, but it's always good to keep such large numbers in perspective. In 2003, the entire U.S. economy produced $11 *trillion* of products and services.[2] So the $500 billion trade deficit was 4.5% of the U.S. economy—a significant but not overwhelming part of the economy.

The main argument used against a trade deficit is that it costs our country jobs and income. That is, if the trade deficit of $500 billion had been spent on products and services from companies in the United States, those companies would have needed to hire more workers and pay more wages and salaries.

In fact, four centuries ago some people espousing a philosophy called "mercantilism" went a step further.[3] They said the key to a country's prosperity was to export as much as possible and to import as little as possible—that is, to run a big "trade surplus."

Although this idea may have much appeal to you, let me poke some holes in it. A large part of our trade deficit is from importing over half our oil needs. The United States actually has large supplies of oil buried underground and off the coastline. Following the mercantilism philosophy, we should stop importing oil and pump all our oil from domestic sources. Maybe we should even try to export oil.

But what if pumping oil domestically is more expensive than importing oil? What if Middle East oil is cheaper to obtain because it's very close to the surface, whereas U.S. oil is expensive to get at because it is far underground or far underwater? Then cutting ourselves off from foreign oil would actually cost us more and make gasoline more expensive.

Actually the situation described above is, indeed, the case. Middle East oil is cheaper to pump than U.S. oil, and that's why we buy it.[4] Buying gasoline refined from Middle East oil saves money for motorists, and this improves our standard of living.

So a trade deficit isn't bad if it results from U.S. consumers and businesses buying foreign-made products that are cheaper or of better quality than their domestic counterparts. The money U.S. consumers and businesses save as a result can be spent on other products and services, many of which may be made in the United States.

But what about those lost jobs and income resulting from a trade deficit? Well, there's good news here also. The dollars accumulated by foreign companies and individuals from the trade deficit aren't lost in space or hoarded. They actually return to the United States in the form of investments. That's right, foreign companies and individuals will invest their dollars in U.S. stocks, bonds, land, companies, farms, and factories. In any year, there's almost an exact identity between the trade deficit and the net investment by foreigners in the United States.[5]

And guess what? Those foreign investments in the United States create U.S. jobs and income. Look at all the foreign auto, tech, and electronics factories built in the United States during the past twenty years. It's no coincidence this has occurred at the same time the United States has run a trade deficit. And those factories pay salaries to thousands of U.S. workers.

Of course, the jobs created by foreign investments aren't necessarily the same as the jobs lost from the trade deficit. But recently, they've actually been better. Much of the foreign investment has gone into auto plants and high-tech firms, both of which pay top-dollar salaries. In contrast, many of the jobs lost from the trade deficit have been lower-paying textile and apparel positions.

One potential "downside" some may see to the foreign investment created by a trade deficit is the resulting increase in foreign ownership of U.S. property, land, companies, and stock. Regardless of whether this is a problem, foreign ownership and control of U.S. assets are still relatively small. Foreigners have owned about 1% of U.S. farmland for almost twenty years, and foreign ownership of other U.S. assets stands at less than 10%.[6] And this doesn't even account for U.S. ownership of foreign assets.

Smart Economics realizes trade deficits are not all bad. While trade deficits do cost the United States jobs and income, the foreign investment caused by the deficits creates jobs and income in our country. Plus, if U.S. businesses and consumers purchase foreign-made products and services because they're cheaper or better than their U.S.-made counterparts, then this is a benefit for the U.S. economy, not a loss.

30 Is a "Strong" Dollar Good and a "Weak" Dollar Bad?

Although most words in the English language have multiple meanings, popular usage often assigns only one definition to each word. So when people hear the word *strong,* they think "good, solid, beneficial," and when they see *weak,* they translate "bad, fragile, failing" (except for some teenagers today, who have reversed the standard meanings of *good* and *bad,* but that's another story!).

Therefore, when someone hears "strong dollar" or "strengthening dollar," they immediately think this is a good thing, and when they hear "weak dollar" or "weakening dollar," they think it's bad. Even news reporters will communicate these interpretations with their intonation or rise of the eyebrows!

But if there's only one thing economics teaches us, it's this: The economic world is full of trade-offs, and for every plus there's a minus, and for every benefit there's a cost.

Perhaps nowhere is this truer than with *exchange rates*, which is what we're talking about with a "strong" or "weak" dollar. The dollar's exchange rate translates dollars into foreign currency. When the dollar strengthens, this means you get more units of foreign currency in trade for a dollar, and when the dollar weakens, you receive fewer units of foreign currency in trade for a dollar.

Now, at first glance, you might think it's better to have a strong dollar, because this means when you exchange dollars for foreign currency, you'll get more of the foreign money and therefore be able to buy more foreign products. And indeed you are correct. A stronger dollar makes foreign travel cheaper and makes purchases of foreign-made products less expensive.

But if a stronger dollar makes foreign-made products cheaper, this means foreign imports are cheaper. So U.S. consumers will buy more foreign imports with a stronger dollar. Also, a stronger dollar makes U.S.-made products more expensive in foreign countries, so this hurts U.S. exports to other countries. The net result: A stronger dollar means U.S. exports drop, foreign imports into the United States rise, and the trade deficit widens.

Now, as I discussed in Chapter 29, a trade deficit isn't the "big bad wolf" that some worry about. But it's interesting to realize that one consequence of a stronger dollar is a bigger trade deficit. So if you are one of those who worry about a trade deficit, you shouldn't be in favor of a stronger U.S. dollar.

What about the flip side—a weaker dollar? Here, the effects are just the opposite of a stronger dollar. A weaker dollar makes foreign travel more expensive and also increases the cost of foreign imports. Yet at the same time a weaker dollar reduces the cost of U.S. exports in foreign countries. So a weaker dollar decreases foreign imports into the United States, increases U.S. exports to foreign countries, and therefore either reduces the trade deficit or turns the trade deficit into a surplus. Thus, those who like smaller trade deficits or trade surpluses should cheer a weaker dollar.

Is there a "right" or "correct" value for the dollar? That is, should we want a stronger or weaker dollar? The answers are no and no. The dollar's value against foreign currencies is a price, just like the price of eggs, the price of sweaters, or the price of chewing gum. And just as there are no right or correct prices for eggs, sweaters, and chewing gum, there's no right or correct price for the dollar.

Instead, what economists can say about the dollar's value against foreign currencies is that it will respond to the economic fundamentals of supply and demand. Just like when there's a bumper crop of apples, the price of apples falls, so too an increase in the supply of dollars will reduce the dollar's value. Likewise, when something motivates people to purchase more apples, the price of apples rises; similarly, anything that increases the demand for dollars—that is, anything that increases the desire of people to have dollars—will increase the dollar's value.

Many, many factors can influence the supply and demand for dollars, but three very important ones are international uncertainty, economic growth, and inflation. Given the United States's "superpower" status in the world, anything that increases international fear and uncertainty tends to increase foreigners' desire to hold dollars, and consequently the dollar's value rises.

Similarly, if economic growth in the United States is stronger than economic growth in foreign countries, then more people will want to use dollars rather than other currencies in economic exchanges, and the dollar's value will increase. Conversely, slower economic growth in the United States will reduce the use of dollars compared to foreign currencies, and the dollar's value will fall.

Last, the dollar's value will be influenced by inflation in the United States compared to inflation in other countries. Higher inflation means the government is printing more of its currency. So if inflation in the United States is higher than inflation in foreign countries, then more dollars are being printed compared to the printing of foreign currencies. This makes each dollar worth less compared to a unit of foreign currency, so the dollar's value falls. The opposite situation also holds. If U.S. inflation moves lower than foreign inflation, then the dollar's value jumps.

So there you have it—the fundamentals of the dollar's exchange rate. I think you'll agree that it's much more than saying, "A strong dollar is good and a weak dollar is bad."

Smart Economics realizes two important facts about the dollar's value relative to foreign currencies. First, this "exchange rate" is a "price" just like the price of a loaf of bread or the price of a gallon of gasoline. Many factors, most of them beyond the government's direct control, influence this price. Second, there are benefits and costs to both a "strong" dollar and a "weak" dollar. Some people and some economic sectors benefit from a strong dollar, whereas other people and other economic sectors do better with a weak dollar.

31 Are Profits Bad?

To many, *profit* is a "dirty" word. It represents the "greed" of business owners. It also represents a cost paid by consumers for which they receive no corresponding benefit. That is, if profits didn't exist, prices could be lower and consumers could lead richer and happier lives.

But I want to convince you that profits are really the consumer's best friend and that without profits prices would actually be *higher* and products and services would be poorer. To do this, this chapter will be a little longer than the others, but I hope you'll agree it's worthwhile because the role of profit is very much misunderstood.

To understand the important role played by profits in our economy, let me take you back to your childhood. As children, most of us hated to keep our room picked up (and some of us have maintained this trait as adults!). Your parents may have admonished and cajoled you to keep your room neat and tidy, and perhaps every now and then, when the mood struck, you'd make an effort to please them (but probably not too much effort). And eventually your mom or dad would have had enough and would come in and clean the room themselves. (Maybe then you'd feel a little guilty, but the guilt would quickly pass.)

But then your parents used a little psychology. They offered you this deal: Every week that your room was kept clean and orderly, your parents would pay you $20 (or $10 if you were a child in the 1970s, $5 if you grew up in the 1960s, and $2 for room cleanup in the 1950s—remember inflation!).

You took the deal, and both you and your parents were happy (and all went on to live a long and prosperous life!). You were happy because you got some spending money. Your parents were happy because they got a clean room, and they didn't have to use their precious time to do the work. So the deal was a mutually agreeable trade.

Well, some psychologists say the "child" in us never leaves—we just do a better job of masking it as we age. And just as when you responded to the incentive of payment for keeping your room clean as a child, each of us still responds to incentives in the economic world.

Profit is an *incentive*. The attraction of making profits—that is, revenues greater than costs—is what motivates people to go into business in the first place. Businesspeople (economists call them "entrepreneurs") look around their neighborhood, city, or perhaps the world for opportunities of what people want. People want food, clothes, houses, cars, CDs, movies and sports for entertainment, and so on. OK, businesspeople work hard to put together the commodities, workers, shipping, and servicing that will meet these "wants." And what motivates businesspeople to do all this? It's the incentive of earning "profits," which are the rewards for their hard work.

But how do we know businesspeople will work hard to give consumers what they want? Because if they don't, someone else will do it. In our economy, where the government doesn't tell people what to do, there are millions of people and businesses constantly looking for consumer wants that are going unsatisfied. Businesses producing products and services that satisfy these wants will reap the rewards in the form of profits.

Think of profits as signals. They tell businesses what and where to produce to satisfy consumer wants and needs. And since consumer wants and needs, and the ways to meet those wants and needs, are constantly changing, there's an ever-changing mix in successful businesses. Companies producing computers are today much more successful than those making typewriters.

The lure of profits is what allows our economy, and economies like it, to be largely undirected by the government. For the most part, the U.S. government doesn't tell businesses what to produce, how much to produce, and where to sell their product. The government lets businesses make those decisions, and the attraction of making profits is the guiding hand for businesses. So the government doesn't have to worry about the 100,000 residents of a city going hungry. Farmers, food processors, and supermarkets know there's "money to be made" (i.e., profit) in providing food to the people, and that's why they'll be fed.

Over the centuries, countries have learned that "top-down" control of the economy by the government doesn't work. There's no way a handful of government bureaucrats can replace the motives of millions of profit-driven businesspeople to, first, find out what people want, then deliver it.

Now don't get me wrong. Although businesses give billions annually to charities and "good" causes, at their core, businesspeople aren't motivated by altruism or "doing the right thing," such as feeding people. No, they're motivated by making profits. But the neat thing about this is, the desire by businesspeople to make profits dovetails exactly with the desire of consumers to have their wants and needs met. It's like the old adage, You scratch my back, and I'll scratch yours!

But what about the argument that profit costs consumers money? That is, if a business has to cover its costs *and* make a profit, doesn't this mean prices to consumers will be higher than without the profits?

The answer is no, and it's based on a five-letter word: *waste*. Let's go back to our room-cleaning example. With no monetary incentive for cleaning your room, when the urge did strike you, you'd probably mope around for several hours, picking up a sock here and a shirt there, until maybe an entire afternoon had been frittered away and your room still only looked slightly better. In other words, you wasted a lot of time in your halfhearted room-cleaning effort.

But with the attraction of money being given to you once your clean room met the approval of your parents, you'd probably work like a demon to get the room in spiffy shape in half the time as when you moped around. This is because you were working toward a clear goal you wanted—money. Plus, over time you'd learn those parts of a clean room your parents were most interested in (maybe they especially wanted a clean floor but didn't care if your desk was messy), and so you'd devote more of your efforts to those parts of the room.

Well, it's the same with businesses. Profit-seeking firms actually cost consumers *less* for two reasons: Profit-seeking firms work hard to eliminate waste, and they work hard to give consumers what consumers want. Profit-seeking firms are constantly "tweaking" their products and production methods to see if they can reduce costs without hurting customer satisfaction, or to see if they need to add a feature that consumers want and are willing to pay for. If a company doesn't do these things, they'll lose sales and maybe be out of business because some competing company will.

The ability of profit-making companies to reduce waste and costs, and therefore prices, is one reason why they usually run rings around nonprofit government providers when they go head-to-head for the consumer's dollar. Without the goal of profits to guide them and the threat of competitors to take away their business, government managers don't have the same motivation to cut waste and push workers to keep customers happy.

In fact, the government-run post office has only recently improved its attention to costs and service with the advent of private alternatives to mail delivery. And in some states, private prison operators and private garbage collection firms are used rather than government-run operations because the private firms are cheaper for taxpayers. Also, a big part of the debate over school vouchers and private schools versus public schools is whether introducing profits and competition to K–12 education would eliminate waste and improve outcomes for parents and students.

But doesn't all this praise for profit mean that if something isn't profitable, it won't be provided by businesses, and as long as something is profitable—no matter how disgusting—it will be provided? Yes, it certainly does, and this does raise some issues.

If a particular product or service is only desired by a few number of people, or if people aren't willing to pay enough to cover the costs and profits needed to provide the product or service, then that product or service won't be offered by private businesses. Businesspersons would say, "There's no money in it." And you can understand the reasoning of business. Again, businesses aren't charities. Their purpose is to make things that consumers want and that earn the business a profit.

But this does produce an issue for government, because in these cases it's usually government that is asked to subsidize or fully pay for the provision of the unprofitable product or service. And then government officials must ask themselves whether there's some broad, socially redeeming feature of the product or service that justifies taxpayer support, or whether there's simply "no market" for it.

Symphonies are good examples. In most cities and states that have symphonies, they are partially funded by taxpayers. That is, people who attend the symphonies don't pay for their full costs. Supporters of public support say symphonies serve a broad social role by preserving the playing of classical music and exposing schoolchildren, especially, to this music. Skeptics say the support of tax money is simply a backdoor way of getting people who could care less about classical music to subsidize those who do.

And what about the profit motive promoting "disgusting" products and services, such as, some would say, pornography, tobacco products, recreational drugs, and "offensive" music? Isn't this the evil side of profit?

No, if anything, the making and marketing of these products represent the evil side *of us*. If the above cited products and others are "evil," "disgusting," or "revolting" (and *I'm* not necessarily saying they are—I have my own opinions, but you'll have to decide for yourself), they exist only because enough people want them and are willing to pay for them. In addition to not being charities, businesses are also not moral compasses. If enough people want something and are willing to pay the costs, some businesses will provide it. But this does present another sticky issue for government between preserving the rights of citizens to pursue their own interpretation of happiness and the desire of other citizens to be protected from possible negative side effects of such pursuits. And this is "way beyond" my abilities.

Smart Economics knows the important role of profits in our economy. When combined with competition, the seeking of profits causes businesses to deliver what consumers want but at the lowest cost. Yet this does mean unprofitable products won't be available unless helped by government or charities, and everyone won't like everything that is provided in the marketplace.

32 Does Business Make Obscene Profits?

Many, many, many (OK, enough) years ago while I was in college, I worked part-time at a furniture store. Nothing glamorous—I worked as a warehouse assistant and spent most of my time moving chairs, sofas, lamps, and wood pieces from the warehouse to the display floor and sometimes to buyers' homes.

Occasionally the owner would let me unpack a new shipment of, say, lamps and price them. The pricing rule he gave me was this: Take the wholesale price (the price the owner paid), double it, and then add another 20%.

I thought to myself, Wow, the owner is making a gigantic profit! (And at the same time, I asked myself, Why am I making only $1.65 an hour?) If he pays $20 for a lamp and sells it for $48, no wonder the owner drives a Cadillac. It sure would be nice to be the owner of a furniture store and make a profit of over 100%.

Perhaps you think the same thing. Most of us are not business owners. Yet most of us would love to be a "boss" because we think the bosses make big profits.

Now, years later, I know how naive I was about the furniture store. Sure, the owner marked up the price he paid for the furniture by 120%. But out of this 120%, he had to pay a boatload of costs before keeping anything for himself. He had to pay such costs as employee salaries and benefits, rent or payments on his building and equipment, insurance on the furniture in the case of fire, advertising, utility costs for lighting, heating, and cooling, and cleaning services (customers don't like to see dusty furniture).

And don't forget taxes. The owner paid local property taxes and business fees and permits, state income taxes, federal income taxes, and FICA (Social Security and Medicare) taxes on his employees.

Plus there were two hidden costs that may not have shown up on any accountant's books but were economic costs nevertheless. One was the cost of the owner's personal time. I'll bet the furniture store owner was at the store sixty to seventy hours a week. Yet he didn't draw a salary, so there was no salary for him on the books. Still, this didn't make his time worthless. On the contrary, the furniture store owner was a smart person, who could have earned a decent salary working sixty to seventy hours somewhere else. So the salary he could have earned in another job should be considered an economic cost.

Second, at any point in time the furniture store owner probably had a couple of million dollars worth of furniture in the warehouse, either awaiting sale or delivery. Again, this money, if not tied up in the furniture, could have been invested by the owner and earned some financial return. This foregone financial return was another cost.

So when all these costs are recognized, how much profit do business owners make? Not accounting for the value of the owner's time, the answer is approximately 7%.[1] That is, out of every dollar in receipts, the average business keeps about 7 cents in profit.

But this 7% is really too high because of inflation. Huh? Well, here's what I mean. Think of yourself as an investor. Say you invest some money in a bank CD and earn 5%. Yet if prices went up an average of 2% during the year (the inflation rate was 2%), then your *real* (after-inflation) investment return is only 3%. In other words, 2% of your 5% return simply let you keep up with higher prices—allowed you to tread water, so to speak. This is the way financial experts look at investments all the time. They look at what they've earned *after* subtracting inflation.

Well, this principle also applies for businesses. After all, a business is really an investment for its owners. When inflation is taken out of profits, the average profit rate over the past fifty years falls to only 3%![2]

Just think about that: For all the headaches associated with running a business, the benefit all comes down to 3 cents on a dollar of profit. And this profit rate isn't even guaranteed. Both small and big businesses go bankrupt every year. Maybe we should all hug a business owner and thank him or her for taking the risk to provide us with products and services.

Smart Economics knows businesses face a large number of costs and uncertainties that cut into their profits. Rather than double- or triple-digit profit rates, the average business earns a profit rate of less than 10% and less than 5% if inflation is taken into account. The average college student makes a higher profit rate on his or her investment in a degree!

Does Big Business Control the Economy?

Hollywood has a great deal of influence over our lives. Not only do we sit for hours in front of TV and movie screens for entertainment, but many (dare I say "most") people form their perceptions about how the economy works from TV programs and big screen movies.

A common theme running through Hollywood productions is that "big business" controls the economy. Movie and TV scripts like to portray "David and Goliath" situations where the little David—often a worker or consumer—is pitted against the big, bad Goliath—namely, big business. After being wronged and almost beaten down early in the drama, the little David will ultimately triumph over big business and win justice for all (and, of course, all of this happens in the course of thirty minutes or, at most, two hours!).

Or another story line has a small, family-run business being unfairly challenged by big business. Big business will slash its prices and take losses in order to bankrupt the small "mom and pop" store. And if that doesn't work, big business may resort to some underhanded and even illegal methods. Sometimes big business will win in these scenarios, and if it doesn't, it's only because of the swift intervention of some hero or heroine.

Of course, in real life there aren't heroes and heroines always ready and willing to help. So does this mean that in real life big business usually wins and ends up controlling the marketplace?

I suspect many of you will answer yes. After all, except in fiction, won't "big" always win over "little"? In short, isn't it a no-brainer that big business controls the economy?

Well, not so fast. Look at Table 7. It shows the percentage of sales in an industry accounted for by the four largest companies, the eight largest companies, the twenty largest companies, and the fifty largest companies in the country.

TABLE 7. Percentage of Sales Accounted for by the Largest Firms

Industry	4 Largest Firms	8 Largest Firms	20 Largest Firms	50 Largest Firms
Utilities	14.7	22.9	40.6	64.5
Manufacturing	n.a.	n.a.	n.a.	23.0
Wholesale Trade	6.2	8.5	12.9	20.3
Retail Trade	7.9	11.7	18.5	25.7
Transp./Warehse.	11.0	14.5	21.8	30.7
Information	42.9	53.3	65.2	76.1
Finance	6.9	11.8	22.6	38.6
Real Estate	5.3	9.6	14.1	19.5
Professions	4.2	6.8	11.6	16.2
Administration	5.7	8.7	14.2	22.1
Education	8.9	13.2	19.5	26.2
Health Care	6.0	8.1	12.2	17.7
Entertainment	6.6	9.4	14.1	20.6
Hotels and Food	6.5	9.8	14.8	21.1
Other	3.7	5.7	9.4	14.5
Total Economy	n.a.	n.a.	n.a.	26.2*

n.a. = not available.
*Weighted average based on industry sales.

Source: U.S. Bureau of the Census, based on 1997 data, http://www.census.gov.

The numbers are eye-opening. With the exception of two industries, utilities and information, even the fifty largest firms usually account for less than a third of sales. For the entire economy, the fifty largest companies make only 26% of sales. I'd hardly call this dominating. And the percentages are even smaller as the number of companies is reduced. So it's just flat wrong to say a handful of companies control the economy and make most of the sales to consumers.

There are some special factors going on in utilities and information that may explain their high percentages. The utility industry is largely a regulated monopoly, where state governments restrict the number of firms and control competition. The percentages in the information industry are pushed up by the broadcasting sector, which is adjusting to rapidly changing technology and nationwide—even worldwide—standardization in tastes and products.

Of course, in some local or specialized markets, there may be domination by one or a couple of firms in certain sectors of industries. Air transportation is a good example, where one carrier or a few carriers may dominate the flights originating in a local market. Passenger cruise ships are an example of a specialized market where only eight companies control almost 90% of the sales.

But overall it looks like competition reigns and big business doesn't. Economists have also looked at the alleged big business domination of the economy over time. Their conclusion: Big business "control" has not increased and, by some measures, has decreased.[1] The general conclusion is that the fifty largest companies have, at most, control over one-fifth to one-fourth of the economy.

Smart Economics warns against basing your economic beliefs on movie and TV program plots. They're meant to entertain, not educate. The American economy is still dominated by intense competition from many companies. At most, big business (liberally defined to include the fifty largest firms in any industry) controls one-fourth of the economy. And there's no evidence that the economic power of big business has increased over time. If anything, with inexpensive and rapidly changing technology and markets, small businesses can often change and adapt better than big business.

34 Can Pro Sports Teams and Facilities Hit Economic Home Runs?

Although I've used a baseball analogy in the title, I'm really talking about all professional sports and their stadiums and arenas. The issue is whether pro teams and their facilities can dramatically improve the economy in a local area.

If you're even a casual sports fan, I'm sure you know what I'm talking about. A city is trying to lure a pro team or is trying to keep an existing team. But to get or keep the team, the team's owner says he needs a new stadium or arena. And guess who's asked to pony up some or all of the money? Not the owner or the players (all millionaires)—but all residents of the city whether or not they ever go to a game.

But before the masses rebel at this thought, team boosters and backers say, "Wait, this isn't robbing the poor and middle class to help the rich." Instead, the boosters and backers have an economic study showing that the pro team and its spanking-new facility will actually benefit *everyone* in the city. In fact, such studies typically show every dollar of tax money spent building a new stadium or arena results in $3 to $4 of economic gains in the city.[1] And on top of this, boosters and backers say that having or keeping a pro team with a modern playing field will put the city in a "major league" category.

So if these studies are to be believed, pro teams and their facilities are forces of economic development for cities. In short, pro teams create income not just for their owners and players but also for cities and their residents.

Or do they? The benefits of pro teams and their facilities are based on an analysis that goes like this. Take all the spending by fans at the home games of the pro team. Include not only spending on tickets but also on food, parking, and souvenirs. Apply a "multiplier" to this total spending to account for the respending of the money in the city. Typically the multiplier is in the range of 2 to 4. Then, "boom"—this is the economic benefit of the pro team and the team's facility.

The economic studies released by pro team boosters and backers are paid for by those boosters and backers. And guess what? I don't know of any such study that fails to find large economic benefits associated with the pro team!

But that's OK. We'd expect supporters to issue a supporting study. And once the studies are released, they are free to be criticized and picked apart by opponents. This is the "American Way"—a clash of ideas and numbers.

Well, I have to be honest here. I tend to side with the critics of studies claiming big economic benefits from pro sports teams. I (and others) think there are three big problems with the studies.

First, the studies fail to account for the fact that most families have a limited amount of money to budget to "fun" or leisure. So if a city doesn't have a pro sports team for families to spend money on, that family will likely spend their fun money on something else—movies, eating out, shopping at the mall, and so on. So a large part of the spending at the pro games would have been spent anyway in the city—but just on something else.

Second, the multipliers applied to the fan spending assume the recipients of the spending (team owners, players, ushers, food service workers) will turn around and respend the money in the city. Although some will (ushers, food service workers), the big bucks go to the players and owners. And there's no assurance the players and owners will respend the money in the city. Many of them don't even live in the city. Many of the players also funnel a big part of their salaries to investments that can be anywhere in the country or world. At least half the money spent by fans immediately "takes flight" and leaves the city and isn't even available to be respent.

Third, the studies fail to recognize a key principle of economics that can never be escaped: There's no free lunch. This means there are always other ways to spend money, and the foregone benefits from those alternative ways of spending should be considered as costs.

Let's say a city spends $100 million of tax money on a new stadium. The point is, that $100 million could have been spent on new roads, on mass transit, on school buildings, or it could have been given back to citizens, and they could have spent it on food, clothes, cars, furniture—whatever. The potential benefits from these other ways of spending the $100 million should be counted as a cost of the new stadium or arena. Unfortunately, the studies don't do this.

Even if pro team supporters conceded all three criticisms, they could still claim using tax money to help pro teams is worthwhile because the image of a "major league city" will lead to new businesses and faster economic growth. Unfortunately, there's no evidence to support this claim. I analyzed economic growth rates of forty-six cities in the 1990s. I found educational achievement and public spending on police contributed to faster economic growth, while a major league sports team actually caused economic growth to be lower.[2] This makes sense if tax money that cities divert to helping a pro team could have been better spent on other things (education, roads, police) that contribute to economic growth directly. Other studies have found similar results.[3]

Some studies claim the stadiums and arenas for pro teams benefit communities by increasing the property values of homeowners.[4] The argument is that pro teams are an amenity valued by a large number of fans. Fans will therefore want to live in cities with pro teams, so they will be willing to pay more for homes in such cities.

While feasible, this line of thought ignores the fact that probably even more people value good schools, good roads, and safe and secure neighborhoods. So, again, spending the money used to subsidize stadiums and arenas on schools, roads, and public safety would likely enhance property values even more.

Don't get me wrong: I'm not an anti-sports person. In fact, I'm a big, big major league baseball fan (for a team playing its home games on the Ohio River across from Kentucky), and I also have favorites in the other pro leagues. So from a personal, selfish point of view, I like attending games in new facilities that other people have paid for.

But when I put on my public policy hat, I have to say that spending taxpayer money on subsidizing pro sports teams and building new stadiums and arenas is not a good idea from the point of view of the entire city economy. Sure, the team owners, players, stadium/arena workers, and surrounding landowners and businesses may benefit, but the wider economy does not.

Smart Economics knows that studies touting the tremendous economic benefits of pro sports teams and their facilities are seriously flawed. Few other industries siphon money *out* of a local area like pro sports. There's also no economic bump from being a "major league city." Cities may still want to court major league teams and subsidize their playing fields, but they shouldn't do it on economic grounds.

35 Why Are Pro Sports Stars Paid So Much for Playing a Game?

Once a month I do a radio call-in show in North Carolina on which I discuss economic topics of current interest. I've been doing this program for almost twenty-five years, and there's one thing I can count on: If a popular professional sports player has recently signed a large new contract, I'll get many callers complaining that the pro star is getting too much money for playing a game, while other workers doing far more important jobs, like police officers, nurses, and teachers, are not paid enough. How, the caller asks, can this be justified?

This really illustrates a love-hate relationship many of us have with celebrities, such as professional sports players and movie and TV stars. On the one hand, we'll go to every game featuring our favorite player, buy replicas of his jersey and team hat, watch every movie and TV show of our favorite actor or actress, and buy every magazine with an article about him or her. But, on the other hand, we'll complain the star makes too much money.

But that's just it. The star makes a lot of money because people willingly spend money at the star's performances (whether on the field or screen) and on products about the star or endorsed by the star. So it's precisely fans who create the conditions for the big paydays earned by big named stars.

All right, let's introduce some economics here. The pay earned by a worker, whether that person is a baseball star or a fast-food worker, is importantly based on two factors. First is the revenue the worker can earn for the business. The more revenue a worker is responsible for earning, the more the business will be willing to pay the worker.

Second is the number of people who can do a particular kind of useful work. The fewer people who can do a particular kind of useful job, the fewer options companies will have in finding workers for that job, and the more they will have to pay each worker.

Understanding how these two factors interact can explain much about pay scales. Combine a job where the worker generates a large amount of revenue for the business *and* where few people can do this job and "shazam" (to quote Gomer Pyle)—you have workers earning big, big, big paychecks. But at the other end of the scale, combine a job where the worker generates little revenue *and* where many, many people can do the job, and you have workers earning tiny paychecks.

Workers earning moderate pay will be in two other categories—(1) jobs where the worker makes a large amount of money for the company but where many people can do the job (2) and jobs where the worker makes little money for the business but where few people can do the job.

Now you can see (I hope) why pro sports and movie and TV stars make so much money. On the one hand, they can generate a gigantic amount of money for the team or studio they work for. Look at home-run king Barry Bonds. His presence on the San Francisco Giants makes the team more exciting and successful. This means more fans in the stands, bigger payments from advertisers and media contracts, and more Giants merchandise sold. All this puts more money in the Giants' coffers, and if, for example, the Giants estimate Bonds's revenue impact to be $25 million annually, he is a bargain for them at a yearly salary of $15 to $20 million.

Or consider movie star Julia Roberts, who reportedly earns $25 million per picture. Although critics may disagree about her acting ability, she nevertheless has established an identity and loyal following that causes most of her movies to gross over $100 million and makes them very profitable for the production studio.

Pro sports and movie and TV stars also benefit from the fact that very few people can do what they do. Although many males have illusions of playing baseball like Barry Bonds, the reality is they can't. Very, very few people, even in their prime, can hit a ninety-mile-an-hour fastball. The same is true of all the professional sports. And while acting ability and popularity are more subjective, once a person has established himself or herself as a box-office star, he or she has no perfect substitute. That is, there may be other actresses who are similar to Julia Roberts, but there is only "one" Julia Roberts, and movie studios know this.

Now, skill and fame can be fleeting and unpredictable, so certainly pro teams and movie executives can make contract mistakes. The sports world is littered with examples of big-name players (at the time) who signed big contracts, and then their performance and revenue-generating ability went downhill (do I hear Ken Griffey Jr., mentioned?). And the popularity and moneymaking machine of Hollywood stars can leave just as quickly as it came. Yet all this illustrates is that forecasting the public adulation and gate or box-office receipts attributed to "stars" is not flawless.

I've given this explanation for the multimillion-dollar salaries of sports and media stars several times to my wife, who happens to be an elementary school teacher. She understands it but still doesn't like it. She still thinks it isn't "fair" that people with less education than her, and doing something that is less "valuable" to society, gets paid so much more than she does.

Of course, to preserve our marriage, I usually nod to my wife and mumble something along the lines, "You're right, dear." But secretly I really want to respond to her this way: Each of us has our own definition of fairness, and it's also natural we all think we're underpaid. What matters to a company about an employee is how much that employee effectively earns for the company. Employees that make more money for the company, regardless of their education, are more "valuable" and will be paid more, especially if there aren't ready replacements who have the same success.

Furthermore, three factors hurt teachers and their salaries. Number one, although no one can deny teaching is an important profession, a large number of people have the talent and capability to become teachers. There are thousands, perhaps millions, of people who have the ability to teach for every person who can hit or throw a ninety-mile-per-hour fastball or shoot a three-point jumpshot with a hand in his face. The same is the case for other "underappreciated" occupations, such as nurses and police officers.

Number two, while pro teams and movie studios can estimate the revenue-generating ability of "stars" and then use these estimates in their salary offers, it's tough—indeed, virtually impossible—for schools to estimate the contribution of teachers to the future financial success of students. Say Mrs. Walden works very hard in helping Timmy pass third-grade math. No one knows what this means for Timmy's future occupation and salary. (Interestingly, college teachers are paid more than elementary teachers, one reason being the more direct link between the educational achievement of college students and their future salaries.)

And number three, sports and media stars shop their skills and talents among many teams and studios. Prior to the 1970s, a player was contractually tied to one team for life or until the team traded the player. This was changed with the advent of "free agency," and once baseball players were able to shop themselves among competing teams, player salaries exploded. This ensures that the teams and studios compete for the stars and pay them what they are worth in terms of their revenue-generating ability.

In most localities, teachers don't have the same ability to shop themselves among competing school districts. In fact, in some areas there is only one county-wide school system, and in some states, teacher salaries are the same statewide. Increasing the competition between public schools for teachers as well as for students would likely improve the salaries of the best teachers.

Let me conclude by tackling the high pay of one other category of workers—CEOs of large corporations. Some claim the millions paid to CEOs is unfair when it's the average worker on the assembly line or in the office that really makes the company go.

Again, I won't attempt to change anyone's notion of fairness, but I will give an economic explanation of why CEOs are paid big bucks. It relates, once more, to revenue and availability. The decisions of CEOs affect a tremendous amount of revenues for the corporation. And in terms of availability, there are a relatively few number of people who have the skills, training, and personal traits to be a successful CEO.

Then why, you might ask, do CEOs continue to earn large salaries—and they may even get bonuses—when the corporation is losing money? Because the owners of the company (shareholders) have decided the company may have lost even *more* money without the good decisions of the CEO. So losing less is the same as earning more.

Smart Economics knows people aren't paid what you or I think they should be but what the "market will bear." This means people in occupations that generate a large amount of revenue for the employer, and in which there are few people who can do the work, will be paid the most. Pro sports and TV and movie stars fit this bill. If you don't like this, then don't buy things that become the revenue behind the stars' salaries.

36 Are We Running Out of Farmers, Farmland, and Soon, Food?

Drive around any major city in the country and what do you see? New housing developments and shopping centers sprouting up like corn. In fact, they're being built where corn used to grow, and this is the alleged problem. It seems as if we're steadily losing farmland. Plus, very few people are going into farming. So, are we on the verge of running out of farmers, farmland, and ultimately, food? Will we soon have to import food, just like we import oil?

No, we won't, but as a verbose economist, I have to explain. The fear about running out of farmland, farmers, and eventually food is a great example of confusing inputs and outputs. Any output is made by combining several inputs. So corn is produced by combining inputs like seed, land, rainfall, fertilizer, machinery, labor, and knowledge. Reduced use of any one input doesn't necessarily mean output will fall. Output can still rise if other inputs are increased.

This is exactly what has happened to farming and food. We certainly have fewer people working on the farm today. Farm labor dropped 70% from after World War II to 2001.[1] But farm output, including both crops and livestock, increased almost 150% over a similar time period.[2] These trends are shown in Figure 11.

How can this be? How can we produce more than double the food with only 30% of the farmers? Well, one reason is that despite all the construction of houses and stores during the past fifty years, the amount of land devoted to farming has not decreased much. In 1999, there was only 16% less land devoted to farming as fifty years earlier.[3]

But more important, other inputs into producing food have increased to more than counteract the decline in farm labor. Farmers today use more and better equipment. A modern tractor can cultivate an acre of land in

FIGURE 11. Farm Output Rises as Inputs Fall (1996=100)

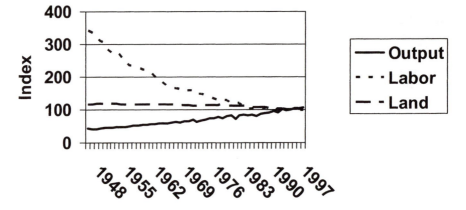

Source: Council of Economic Advisors, *Economic Report of the President, 2004.*

minutes, compared to hours for a mule and plow. Farmers use irrigation systems to counteract droughts and tap into information from satellites to learn about approaching weather patterns. Today's farmer can also plant drought-resistant crops and raise more hearty livestock. Modern farmers have also benefited from advances in controlling plant and animal diseases. Of course, all these technologies, discoveries, and methods weren't even dreamed about fifty years ago.

So the bottom line is that gains in farmer and farmland *productivity* have allowed the U.S. agricultural industry to produce more with the same, or in many cases, more with less. Farmer productivity—how many farm products each farmer is responsible for producing—jumped an incredible 715% between 1948 and 1999, and farmland productivity—how much farm output is produced from each acre of land—rose by almost 200% over the same number of years.[4] And such stellar performance has made the United States a perennial net *exporter* of agricultural products to the rest of the world. The United States truly is the world's breadbasket.

Smart Economics knows it's a mistake to look at inputs and draw an immediate conclusion about output. Despite the tremendous drop in the number of farmers and the modest decline in farmland, U.S. farmers continue to produce more agricultural output each year. The reasons: use of better equipment, better plant varieties and livestock types, control of disease, better adjustment to weather conditions, and smarter farmers. With this combination, there's no reason why American farmers can't continue feeding all of us and much of the rest of the world.

37 Are Gas Prices at an All-Time High?

Many Americans love their cars, and most Americans, even if they don't love their cars, are dependent on them. For better or for worse, over the past fifty years American society has become increasingly oriented around the car (or, to be more technically correct, the car, truck, or sport-utility vehicle [SUV]).

This means most of us buy gas at least once a week, and we therefore watch its price. And even though gas purchases take a relatively small bite out of our budgets, every time the price rises, we yell.[1] We yell that the price is too high and that the gas and oil companies are "taking us for a ride." The media eggs us on by reporting that "gas prices set new highs" and sending out "pump patrols" to find price deals.

So if the price (per gallon) of gas is $2.60 today and five years ago it was $1.40, does this mean gas is more expensive today? Sure, in the sense you have to take more money out of your pocket to buy gas. But what if, as is usually the case, the prices of most things go up over time, including the price of labor, which is the wage rate you and I earn? Then maybe the answer isn't so clear.

I must admit, I'm getting into an area where economists look at prices one way, and most everyone else looks at prices another way. If the price of some item rises, most people will say the item has become more expensive. However, economists will say the item has gotten more expensive only if its price increase was *more* than the price increase of other products and services we buy. Of course, economists think they're right, and I'll try to convince you why.

As I've stated in other chapters, prices tend to march upward over time. Therefore, if everything is moving up in price, we say something is more expensive only if its price has moved up more than the prices of other things. By this reasoning, gas is only getting more expensive if its price has increased faster than the prices of other things we buy.

Look at Figure 12, which shows the price of gas from the late 1950s to 2004. The price of gas in Figure 12 has been—what economists call—*adjusted for inflation*. Essentially this means changes in the price of gas have been adjusted for changes in the average price of all consumer products and services other than energy and food.[2] So the price of gas in Figure 12 only rises if gas prices rise more than the price of other consumer products and services rise. Economists call this the "real" price of gas.

You can see the "real" price of gas has trended downward, with one major exception—the late 1970s and early 1980s. This was the period of the Iranian revolution and oil embargos from oil-producing countries in the Middle East. Even the recent run-up in gasoline prices in 2003 and 2004 was a relatively minor blip. By this measure, the price of a gallon of gasoline in 2004 was 30 cents less than the price in 1959 and $1.23 less than the peak price in 1981.

OK, I understand if you don't totally "buy" this explanation. So let me try it another way. Let's compare the actual price (not the "real" price) of a gallon of gasoline to the average hourly wage rate earned by workers, then calculate how many minutes a person has to work to earn enough

FIGURE 12. Gas Prices Have Edged Lower

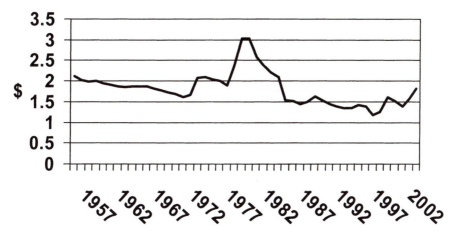

Price per gallon of gasoline expressed in the purchasing power of dollars in 2004 using the core (less energy and food) CPI.

Sources: U.S. Department of Energy, http://www.iea.doe.gov/emeu/steo/pub/fsheets/RealMogasPrices.html; U.S. Bureau of Labor Statistics, http://www.bls.gov.

to buy a gallon of gas. So the "affordability" of gas is measured by how long someone has to work to purchase it.

The answers are in Figure 13, and they are very similar to the conclusions from Figure 12. With the exception again of the 1979–1982 period, gas has become more affordable. In 1959 the average person had to work 9.2 minutes to earn enough to buy a gallon of gasoline. In 2004, this time was down to 6.1 minutes. Since 1959, the least affordable year for gasoline was 1981, when it took 11.1 minutes to earn enough to buy one gallon of gasoline.

Of course, there's no assurance the trend of "cheaper" gas will continue. Some energy analysts think gas prices will begin to rise, over time, with China and other developing countries dramatically increasing consumption and the discovery of large new oil supplies being very uncertain. But if gas does get "pricier," two factors will blunt its effect. One, the higher price will spur the development of affordable alternatives. And two, manufacturers will be motivated to make engines and machines that are progressively more efficient in using gas and oil. Indeed, in the past quarter century, the average energy efficiency of engines and machines doubled.[3] There's no reason why this trend won't continue.

Finally, let me clear up another "mystery" about gas prices. Why is it that gas prices can vary so much geographically on the exact same date?

FIGURE 13. We're Working Less for a Gallon of Gas

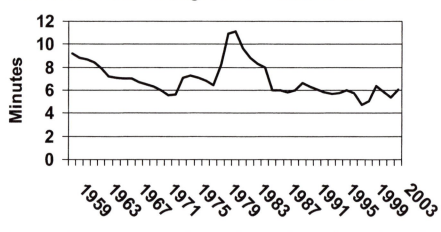

Sources: U.S. Department of Energy; Council of Economic Advisors, *Economic Report of the President, 2004*; author's calculations.

Presumably the price of oil is the same to everyone on the same day, so why shouldn't the price of gas be the same?

Well, one reason could be the price of oil may be different to different suppliers on the same day. For example, some suppliers may have "locked in" a lower price with a long-term contract just before oil prices started to rise. Also, shipping costs are lower near the major Gulf Coast ports, so gas will typically be cheaper in the Southeast, while states with stricter environmental regulations, like California, will certainly have higher gas prices.

But gas prices can vary even within the same city, and sometimes they can be different between a few city blocks. When this happens, it's the result of differences in "demand-side" factors. Gas stations at busier and more convenient locations and those located in more affluent, upscale neighborhoods will be able to charge more to buyers than out-of-the-way stations and stations in poorer neighborhoods.[4]

Smart Economics knows that to determine if a product has become more expensive, its price must be compared to the prices of other products and services or to the wage rate earned by workers. When these measures are made, we find gasoline has not become more expensive. In fact, the average person in 2004 could work 35% less time to earn enough for a gallon of gas as someone in 1959.

38

Do Big Oil Companies Manipulate Oil Supplies and Gas Prices?

I love a good conspiracy as much as the next person. For example, I'm still fascinated by theories and books about who shot JFK. And what about all those supposed UFO sightings? Is there really a warehouse somewhere in the desert with captured alien spacecraft?

There's another favorite conspiracy about the oil market and gas prices, and it goes like this. The big oil companies conspire to manipulate oil supplies in order to keep oil and gas prices high. They may go so far as to keep oil tankers waiting off the coast until the price is high enough for their liking. And once oil and gas prices are high, it takes forever and a day, if ever, for them to come down! In short, big oil companies engage in gas "price gouging."

This sure makes for a good conspiracy, and the story certainly reflects Americans' suspicious feeling toward big business. It also appeals to our desire to have a simple explanation, and someone to blame, for when gas prices rise. But there's one big problem: This conspiracy story is wrong!

Let's start with the claim that once gas prices rise, they rarely come down, and if they do, they fall very, very slowly. The problem with this claim is it flies in the face of the facts. Just look at Figure 14. Two facts jump out. First, gas prices at the pump do go up, and they do go down. They don't stay up once they've risen. Second, there's a close connection between the price of gas at the pump and the price of the raw crude oil. Pump prices rise when crude oil prices rise, and pump prices fall when crude oil prices fall. Research shows the entire change in oil prices, both up and down, is reflected within ten days at pump prices.[1]

So don't blame your local gas station owner or operator when the price of gas goes up. They're simply passing on the higher price of crude oil. And, of course, the reason there's a gap between the price of crude oil and the price of gas at the pump is there are several costs involved in chang-

FIGURE 14. Gas Prices Track Oil Prices

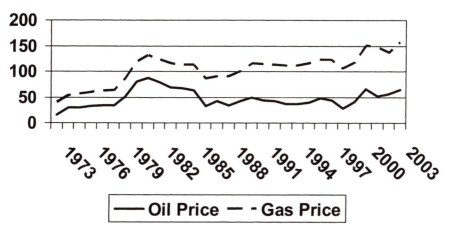

Both prices are unadjusted for inflation.

Sources: Energy Information Agency, *Annual Energy Review, 2002*; Energy Information Agency, *Annual Energy Outlook, 2002*, U.S. Department of Energy, Washington, D.C., December 2001.

ing crude oil into the gas we buy—refining, transportation, marketing, rent, and labor costs, as well as federal and state taxes.

Now, one other observation you can see from Figure 14 is that the gap, or spread, between pump prices and oil prices has widened over time. A big reason for this is federal and state gasoline taxes and the costs of environmental regulations. However, when this spread is adjusted for inflation, it has remained remarkably constant over time.

What about big oil companies conspiring to keep oil and gas prices high? Well, if they are trying to do this, Figure 14, as well as Figures 12 and 13 in the last chapter, show they're not doing a very good job. Both oil and gas prices are more affordable today than they were forty years ago.

If there is a villain in this story, it's not the oil *companies* but some oil-producing *countries*. I'm sure you've heard of OPEC, which stands for the Organization of Petroleum Exporting Countries. OPEC is a "cartel," or "collusive oligopoly" in more technical economics lingo. Cartels cooperate rather than compete. This means they all agree to charge the same price for their product. But to do this, they must limit the total supply of the product, meaning each country agrees to a production limit it won't exceed. Incidentally, cartels are illegal in the United States, but the foreign oil–producing countries aren't subject to U.S. law.

OPEC will try to set the price and production of oil at levels that give them the most profit. This doesn't always mean a higher price, because OPEC knows higher prices can ultimately result in lower sales, and too high of a price can send the buying countries into a recession, which is also bad for OPEC's business.

OPEC also has to contend with two other issues. One is "cheating" by member countries. Countries may be motivated to produce more oil than allotted by the OPEC agreement in order to gain more short-term profits. But this has the effect of increasing total supply, reducing price, and reducing profits for all. Enforcing the production agreements is a continuing problem for OPEC but, of course, a happy circumstance for oil and gas consumers.

The second issue is oil production by non-OPEC nations. Not all oil-producing countries are members of OPEC. These non-OPEC producers have actually become a greater player in the world oil market. For example, the percentage of oil imports purchased by the United States from OPEC countries has decreased from 71% in 1980 to 53% in 1990 to 40% in 2002.[2] The increased availability of oil supplies from non-OPEC countries obviously reduces OPEC's ability to control world oil prices.

This doesn't mean you should shed a tear for OPEC. They've had oil consumers "over a barrel" for decades. What it does mean is that increased competition among oil-producing companies is one of the best ways of keeping oil and gas prices low.

Smart Economics knows claims of oil companies conspiring to keep oil and gas prices high make for a good story, but they don't match reality. While the ups and downs in gas prices do follow ups and downs in crude oil prices, it's not the oil companies pulling the strings; rather, it's a handful of oil-producing countries called OPEC. But OPEC's power is limited and may be waning. If OPEC increases oil prices too much, it can harm the economies of the oil-buying countries. Also, oil production from non-OPEC countries is taking a greater share of the market.

39 Should We Become Energy Self-Sufficient?

Politicians of all stripes like to proudly proclaim: "If elected, I will work to make America energy self-sufficient." Thunderous applause usually follows. People think that if we produced all of our energy needs from domestic sources, we wouldn't have to worry about OPEC, the Middle East, or any other country or region that sells us oil. We could "thumb our nose" at these foreign producers. Plus, if our path to energy self-sufficiency causes us to use more nonconventional sources, like solar and wind power or hydrogen, then a bonus might be a cleaner environment.

These are nice thoughts, and many people work very hard trying to move us closer to the goal of energy self-sufficiency. And maybe someday it will happen. But the simple reality today is, for most people and businesses, that using nonconventional energy sources or technologies will increase costs and reduce their standard of living.

Some of you are now angry at me because I've been so blunt. But don't be. I'm not anti-environment or anti-clean air or pro-OPEC. Yet as an economist I must identify trade-offs. With what we know and can do now, you will pay more to use unconventional fuels. And while some may be willing to pay more, most Americans aren't, and that's why all but a few of us will continue to fuel our cars with gasoline and heat our homes directly or indirectly with oil, natural gas, coal, or nuclear power.[1]

Solar and wind power just can't compete on price and reliability with conventional home energy systems. While there may be monthly operating savings compared to conventional systems, up-front installation costs are much higher. One estimate puts the total cost per kilowatt hour of solar power to be 2.5 to 12 times that of conventionally produced electricity.[2]

The same is true of today's hybrid cars. The magazine *Consumer Reports*, no friend of "big oil" companies, calculated it would take up to twenty years of fuel savings to cover the extra purchase costs of a hybrid car.[3] And this doesn't account for the significant costs of battery pack replacement.[4]

Interestingly, the greatest interest in and use of solar and wind power came in the late 1970s and early 1980s, precisely when the price of oil and gas skyrocketed. But as oil and gas prices fell in the 1990s, solar and wind power rapidly fell out of favor.

Another alternative energy source, gasohol, suffers from a different issue—whether it actually saves or costs energy to use. Gasohol is fuel made from corn. Politicians and farmers in corn-growing states love gasohol because it means a larger market for corn. But to be marketable, gasohol has always needed large subsidies, or tax favors, from federal and state governments, $1 billion in 2002. One reason may be that gasohol uses more energy than it saves.

That is, when all the energy is tallied that it takes to grow the corn and process it into gasohol, some calculations suggest gasohol actually takes about 70% *more* energy to make than the gasohol produces in usable fuel.[5]

But what about oil? Why do we continue to import foreign oil when there's still plenty of oil here in the United States (including Alaska) and offshore? In fact, the United States is still one of the world's leading oil producers. Couldn't we just pump up production a little bit and then cut ourselves off from foreign oil?

Well, first, we now import half our oil, so it would take more than a "little bump up" to become self-sufficient in oil use.[6] In fact, the known oil reserves in Alaska would only supply the United States with less than a year of oil consumption.[7]

But more fundamentally, foreign oil, especially from the Middle East, is cheaper than U.S.-produced oil. The biggest expense in oil production is getting the oil out of the ground. The farther down in the ground the oil is, the more expensive it is to pump. Oil in the Middle East is very close to the surface; in some areas, it's virtually at the surface. In contrast, most U.S. oil fields are far beneath the surface. So even with the 5,000-mile transit, it's still cheaper to pump and ship Middle East oil to the United States than to use oil pumped in the United States. One estimate puts exploration and production costs at five times higher in the United States compared to the Middle East.[8]

Some say the price of Middle East oil is *artificially* low because it doesn't factor in the security costs to the United States of trying to keep peace in the Middle East. In effect, some folks say Middle East oil is being subsidized by U.S. taxpayers in the form of our large military expenditures associated with that region.

This is a controversial perspective, but I think the folks making it have a point. Adding a "security tax" to gasoline prices would be significant. Depending on how much of our defense budget can arguably be allocated to protecting oil supplies out of the Middle East, a security tax could add between 12 cents and 75 cents to the price of a gallon of gasoline.[9]

Indeed, the best way to reduce fossil fuel (oil, gasoline) consumption would be to significantly increase the tax on those fuels. Politically, however, this doesn't seem possible. Even talk of increasing the federal gas tax by pennies per gallon runs into a buzz saw of opposition. Still, if we were really serious about motivating people to change their driving habits, we'd hit everyone in the pocketbook and wallet.

Smart Economics knows that energy self-sufficiency today would come at a large price. It would cost all of us more to power our homes and fuel our vehicles with unconventional energy sources like solar, wind, and hybrid power and gasohol. Even our domestically pumped oil costs more than foreign-produced oil, and that's why we import over half our oil needs. However, a reasonable question is whether foreign oil gets a free ride because we don't tack on our related military and security costs to each barrel of imported oil. If this were done, gas prices would jump, and alternative energy sources would become much more feasible.

40 Is Immigration Hurting Our Economy?

America has always been the land of opportunity for foreigners, but the gates to immigrants have been wide open in recent years. Immigration reached levels not seen in a hundred years during the 1990s, with 1.3 million legal and illegal immigrants entering the United States each year.[1]

This recent immigration—some term it the "new immigration"—has resulted in many changes. For example, persons of Hispanic background are now the largest minority group in the United States, and Spanish is the second most used language. But some say there's been too much immigration, because, they say, the new immigration has created large social and economic costs.

Yet if there's anything economics teaches us, it is that most issues are a comparison of benefits and costs. So while there may very well be costs from the new immigration, there are also likely to be benefits, and our society much balance the two.

Although some of the concerns about the new immigration are directly related to the number of recent immigrants, there's also the fact that the new immigrants are different than their earlier predecessors. Recent immigrants have lower educational levels and fewer formal skills compared to earlier arrivals and compared to the U.S. population. More of today's immigrants are high school dropouts than a decade ago. And the proportion of recent immigrants who are high school dropouts is three to four times higher than for native persons.[2]

Consequently, the large wave of new immigrants has swelled the numbers of low-skilled and low-wage workers in America. Over 40% of new immigrants earn wages in the bottom 20% of the wage distribution, and today's new immigrants earn over 30% less, on average, than existing U.S. workers.[3]

This is not to say immigrants are worse off in the United States than they would be in their original country. Despite little formal education and low pay, immigrants are probably better off in the United States. But there's a hidden financial impact from the new immigration that imposes a cost on *some* U.S.-born workers while creating a benefit for U.S. consumers.

The financial impact is this: The new immigration has greatly expanded the numbers (or "supply" to use economics lingo) of workers in the country with little formal training and skills. Economics teaches us that when the supply of anything, including workers, increases noticeably, the market value—here the wage rate—falls.

This means the new immigration of large numbers of unskilled and lower-skilled workers entering the country has resulted in lower wages for *all existing* unskilled and lower-skilled workers. Some studies say the new immigration is responsible for a 5% drop in the income of low-skilled workers and for over half of the increased gap in recent years between the earnings of lower-skilled and higher-skilled workers.[4]

This is an important point. Maybe an example will clarify any confusion. Let's say five years ago there were 1,000 people who worked as day laborers at construction sites in a city. Today, as a result of the new immigration, there are 1,500 day laborers, and the amount of work is roughly the same (in economics terms, there's a bigger supply for the same demand). Since there are more workers competing for the same number of jobs—guess what?—construction managers are able to hire each worker for less money than five years ago.

So this is a "cost" of the new immigration to U.S.-born low-skilled workers. But there's a "flip"-side benefit. If the new immigration has pushed down the wages of lower-skilled workers, then this means prices of the products and services made by lower-skilled workers can be sold at lower prices. Consumers, therefore, reap a benefit!

If the calculations of economists studying this impact are to be believed, it can be huge, as high as $150 *billion* annually. Most of this $150 billion is a *transfer* from lower-skilled workers who earn less to consumers who pay less. Maybe 5% of the $150 billion, or $8 billion, represents a net gain to the economy.[5]

Now let's look at the impact of the new immigration on government, for both the cost of government services and government tax revenues.

With a major portion of recent immigrants having limited skills and consequently earning low pay, it should not be surprising that their use of public assistance is greater than for existing U.S. households. Recent data show 22% of immigrant households use some form of public assistance, compared to 15% for the native population.[6]

This finding might suggest immigrants cost the government more than they pay in taxes. And, indeed, some studies find this is the case.[7]

But there's another possibility when the entire work career of immigrants is considered. One well-known potential problem with Social Security is the declining number of workers supporting each retiree. Since Social Security payments to existing retirees depend, in part, on the Social Security taxes paid by current workers, the fewer workers there are for each Social Security retiree, the greater the chance Social Security taxes will have to be increased or benefits cut.

Immigrants increase the pool of workers paying Social Security (and Medicare also) taxes and thus increase the worker/retiree ratio. As a result, some studies find the large recent immigration could actually *improve* the government's fiscal affairs, at least over the next thirty to forty years.[8]

Truly, immigration is more complicated than at first glance. It is a matter of costs and benefits—but, often, to different people!

Smart Economics recognizes immigration is a complex issue because it involves both costs and benefits. In the private economy, the recent large immigration has increased the numbers of low-skilled workers in the country and has depressed the wages of all low-skilled workers; however, it has resulted in lower prices for consumers. For government, the recent immigration has increased costs for public assistance and education. Yet the jury is still out on whether immigrants more than make up for these costs with added tax revenues. When the payroll taxes paid to Social Security and Medicare by immigrants are considered, immigration may actually improve the fiscal balance of government over the next thirty to forty years.

 Economic Questions about How Households Live and How They Earn and Spend Money

41 Is Everything More Expensive Today (or, Should You Wish for the "Good Old Days")?

Most of us can remember when we bought our first car or house. We were shocked at the price, especially after talking to older relatives or friends who told us what they paid for their first car and home. In fact, although people don't track the numbers, there's a feeling that most things tend to get more expensive year after year.

Actually, this "feeling" is correct. The government bean counters who track consumer prices report that, with rare exceptions, an average of all consumer prices rises every year. Sure, there can be differences in how fast prices rise. In the late 1970s, they were rising at double-digit rates, whereas in the late 1990s the annual increase was about 2%; but they have been increases nevertheless.

So does this mean we're all worse off today because everything is more expensive? Absolutely not! What people who wish for the "good old days" forget is that in those days incomes were also lower, and as prices have increased, so too have people's incomes. This actually makes a lot of sense. If businesses are charging higher prices and earning more revenues, they have more money to pay workers.

So what really matters is whether the increase in incomes has kept pace with the increase in prices. To see if they have, look at Figure 15. It compares the increase in consumer prices to the increase in after-tax income per person and to average hourly wage rates over the past five decades. With one exception (wage rates in the 1980s), incomes and wages have more than kept pace with price inflation. So despite the onward march of higher prices, the average household's ability to afford those prices has been maintained.

There is an important caveat to what I've said here. All the statistics are based on "averages." And of course no one is average. Certainly, there are many households in the last five decades whose wages and incomes have

FIGURE 15. Income and Wage Gains Have Outpaced Price Increases

Decade of 2000s spans 1999–2003; price changes are based on the consumer price index.

Source: Council of Economic Advisors, *Economic Report of the President, 2004,* Tables B-31, B-40, B-60.

not kept up with rising prices. But at the same time, there are many households whose increases in wages and incomes have skyrocketed past price hikes. Yet the bottom line is, when an average of all households is taken, we've been able to run past price increases.

Smart Economics knows the important issue is not that everything costs more over time but whether our incomes rise enough to afford the higher prices. Fortunately, the answer is that, for the average household, wages and incomes do increase as fast as (and in most cases, faster than) prices. So— guess what?—the "good old days" are today!

42 Does It Take Two Incomes for Families to Get Ahead Today?

Tune in the TVland cable channel one evening and you'll see sitcoms from the 1950s and 1960s, such as *I Love Lucy, Leave It to Beaver*, and *Bewitched*. It's fun to compare the clothing and hairstyles, the language, and the home appliances to those of today.

Of course, these sitcoms, like those of today, reflect the times. One thing that's evident from the sitcoms of forty and fifty years ago is that wives didn't work. Oh sure, they worked in the home—cleaning, cooking, and taking care of the kids—and don't get me wrong, this is hard and challenging work. But wives then didn't work at a job for pay—or, in the lingo of economics, they didn't work in the "marketplace."

Today is different. In half of married couple families, both husbands and wives work at jobs for pay.[1] Eating meals out is more common than eating home-cooked meals for most families. Day care for young children is a big industry, and cleaning the house is a chore that often falls by the wayside.

What happened? Why are families with both parents working for pay the norm rather than the exception?

The common answer given is, wives *have* to work. With everything costing more today than in the past, most Americans think both the husband and wife have to work to achieve the same living standard as in the 1950s and 1960s when one-worker families were the norm.

But let's not take what "most Americans think" as necessarily the truth. Fortunately, the government has collected statistics over many years on the incomes of families with different numbers of workers.

Figure 16 gives these income statistics for the past fifty-plus years for three types of families: married couple families with the wife working (Cou-WW), married couple families where the wife doesn't work (Cou-NWW), and—because they have increasingly become a significant type of

FIGURE 16. Median Family Income Has Risen for All Households But More for Dual Earners (2001$)

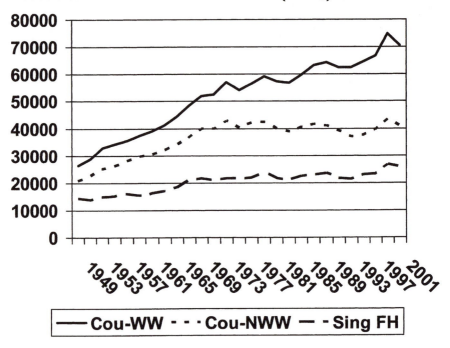

Source: U.S. Bureau of the Census, *Mini-Historical Statistics*, Nos. H2, H25.

family structure—families headed by a female with no husband present (Sing FH).

The dollar values in Figure 16 have also been preadjusted to account for changes in consumer, or retail, prices. That is, for example, if a family's income increased 3% in a year, but consumer prices (or the cost of living) also rose 3%, then no increase in the family's income is recorded. The dollar values are expressed in terms of the purchasing power of dollars in 2001. This puts all the incomes in different years on the same footing in terms of what the incomes can purchase.

So what's really happened to family incomes? Well, the statistics show incomes for the three family categories have *not* gone down. Yes, they do bounce around a little, usually going down during years when the economy is in a recession, but it *can't* be said that families today have less income than in years past, even after accounting for higher prices.

The incomes in Figure 16 actually *understate* how far family income goes in recent years, because families have been getting smaller. Families in 2000 had 17% fewer people than families in 1970 and were 24% smaller than families in 1950.[2] If the incomes in Figure 16 had been expressed on a per person basis, incomes in recent years would be adjusted upward relative to incomes in earlier decades.[3]

The data do reveal one trend that may explain why one-earner families feel as if they've fallen behind families where both the husband and wife work. Although the incomes of one-earner families haven't gone down, the *difference* between their income and the income of two-earner families has widened in recent years. So while the incomes of one-earner families have kept up with rising prices, the incomes of two-earner families have *more* than kept up with the higher cost of living.

And why has this occurred? If you think about it, it doesn't make much sense that the answer would be based simply on the number of workers in the family. It has to be based on the characteristics of the workers and how those characteristics may be different between families with the wife working and families where the wife doesn't work.

A clue appears in Figure 17. It's well known that our economy has become more education-oriented. The knowledge needed to use modern technology has driven up the benefits from education. Figure 17 shows that the incomes (again adjusted to account for higher prices over time) of college graduates have risen since the late 1970s (incomes of college grads fell in the early 1970s as the large "baby boom" class began graduating and swelling the ranks of those with college degrees).

But while those with advanced knowledge have benefited from the knowledge-based economy, those with fewer formal skills and training have fallen behind. Also, those with less education are increasingly finding themselves in direct competition with lower-skilled workers in foreign countries. Consequently, the price-adjusted incomes of high school dropouts and high school graduates have fallen, on trend, since the 1970s, meaning the income gap between college graduates and noncollege graduates has widened in the last thirty years.

OK, but what does this have to do with the growing income gap between two-worker families and one-worker families? Here's what. A much higher proportion of two-worker families have at least one college graduate than do other family types. Almost 37% of families with both the hus-

FIGURE 17. College Graduates Have Gotten Ahead (2001$)

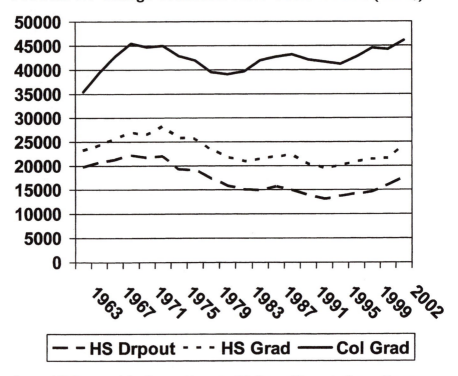

Sources: U.S. Bureau of the Census, *Measuring Fifty Years of Economic Change*, Current Population Reports P60-203, Table C-8 (Washington, D.C.: Government Printing Office, September 1998); and U.S. Bureau of the Census, *Annual Demographic Survey and Economic Supplement*, Current Population Survey (Washington, D.C.: Government Printing Office, September 2003).

band and wife working have at least one of them possessing a college degree, compared to 22% for all other family types.[4]

So if there's a "culprit" for one-earner families, it's education. Fewer of them simply have the education needed to do very well in today's economy. In contrast, more of two-earner families are on the economic fast track because one or both of the workers have college degrees.

There's one more piece to the working wife debate. Some claim that even though today's families may earn more income than earlier families, once taxes and necessities are subtracted, households today have less "leftover," or "discretionary" income. A related concern is that today's two-earner families may actually have less discretionary income than one-earner families once child day-care fees, added spending on clothing, extra transportation expenses (i.e., a second car), and other expenses associated with the second spouse working are subtracted.[5]

While the situations described above are possible, they're not typical. A comparison of a large sample of families in the 1990s compared to families in the 1960s found discretionary incomes increased for both one-earner and two-earner families and for two-earner families in the 1990s compared to one-earner families in the 1960s.[6]

This said, it's still important for two-earner families to make sure they're ahead financially when the added costs associated with the second parent working are identified. Included in these "costs" should be any negative impacts on children's development and educational performance from both parents working. Yet balanced against the costs should be added not only the income from the second worker but also the fringe benefits of any retirement savings and health insurance from the job. It's not an easy comparison!

So why are more wives working today? There are both "push" and "pull" reasons. In families where the husband's price-adjusted income has fallen, wives have been pushed into the workplace in order to keep the family financially afloat. With our changing economy, this is most often the case for husbands without a college degree.

But in other families, the wife has been pulled into working by the increasing work opportunities for women. Said another way, as high-paying professional and managerial jobs have opened for women, particularly for the increasing number of women with college degrees, it's become "too expensive," in terms of the income that would be given up, for some wives to stay home.

Smart Economics knows the key behind a family's economic prosperity is not how many parents work but the educational background of the workers. Average incomes of families with one worker have not dropped in recent decades, but incomes of two-worker families have risen more. The reason is that a much higher percentage of two-worker families have at least one worker with a college degree. And with the modern economy increasing the financial rewards to education, more education is the path to more income.

43

Are Americans Drowning in Debt and Not Saving?

In 2002, the total debt of all American families was over $10 *trillion*.[1] Equally distributed among every man, woman, and child in the country, this came to $36,000 per person. This was 1,100% higher than in 1970 and double the amount in 1990.[2] Even if the dollar amounts are adjusted for inflation (or for the declining purchasing power of the dollar), each person's debt burden was 163% higher than in 1970 and 44% greater than in 1990.

At the same time, Americans don't appear to be saving. The widely publicized "personal savings rate," regularly quoted by the national news media, shows a consistent and steady decline from 8% in the 1980s to only 2% in 2002.[3]

Aren't these numbers clear evidence Americans are drowning in debt and aren't saving for the future? Isn't it just a matter of time before this behavior sinks us? Before you quickly answer yes, let me try to convince you that the commonly quoted numbers on debt and savings leave much to be desired.

Let's take debt first. Suppose the Rogers family owes $100,000 on the home mortgage, car loans, and credit cards. Does this mean they're automatically in financial trouble? Probably so if their annual income is only $25,000, and they have no assets to liquidate to pay off the debt. But probably not if the Rogers family pulls in $250,000 in yearly income and has investments worth $500,000.

The point is, we can't judge debt in isolation. We have to put it in perspective, in terms of either the debt holder's income or the debt holder's investments. More income can support payments on more debt, and more investments can be a counterweight to debt.

Fortunately, we can look at debt in this way, and also study other financial measures, by examining the Federal Reserve System's *Survey of*

Consumer Finances (SCF). The *SCF*, conducted every three years, is the most comprehensive and extensive compilation of financial information on American households.[4]

Figure 18 shows family net worth, which is the difference between the value of a family's investments and the value of its debt. The dollars are again adjusted for inflation, so they are comparable from year to year. The average used is the "median," so it is not distorted, or skewed, by very rich families.[5]

The good news is that for all families the value of investments has more than kept up with the increase in debt. Average family net worth in 2001 was 40% higher than family net worth in 1983. The increase was even more dramatic for college-educated families (up 67%).

But the net worth trends aren't as positive for less-educated and lower-income families. The net worth of high school–educated families and of low-income families was little changed in 2001 from earlier years. And the net worth of families with high school dropouts as workers actually fell over 20% from 1983 to 2001. Some researchers think this is because credit

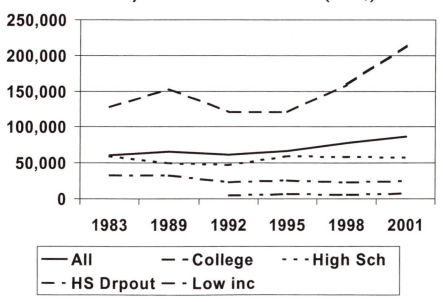

FIGURE 18. Family Net Worth Has Increased (2001$)

Sources: Federal Reserve System, *Survey of Consumer Finances, 1983, 1989, 1992, 1995, 1998, 2001.*

standards have been lowered, making it easier for families traditionally closed out of debt to have access to consumer credit.[6]

Nevertheless, these statistics show the average American family *owns* more than they *owe*. However, a better way to measure the debt burden may be to see how much debt payments—like the home mortgage, car payments, and credit card payments—take from a family's income. The debt payments faced by a family are based not only on the amount borrowed but also on the interest rate charged.

Figure 19 shows trends in debt payments as a percentage of family income, and Figure 20 gives the percentage of families for whom debt payments take more than 40% of their income.

Both trends are amazingly stable. There is a slight up-tick in the percentages in the late 1990s but nothing dramatic with one exception—an increase in debt payment loads for low-income families (Figure 19). However, this percentage dropped back in 2001 almost as much as it rose in 1998.

OK, you say, but what about personal bankruptcies? Aren't they up because of consumer debt?

FIGURE 19. Family Debt Payments as a Percentage of Family Income

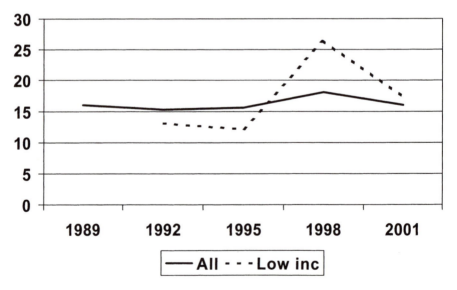

Sources: Federal Reserve System, *Survey of Consumer Finances,* 1983, 1989, 1992, 1995, 1998, 2001.

FIGURE 20. Percentage of Families with Debt Payments Taking More Than 40% of Income

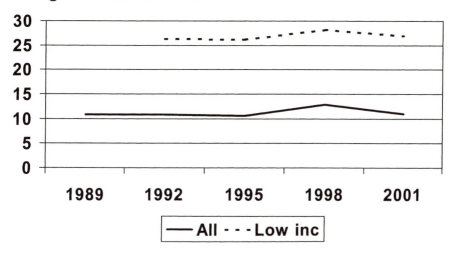

Sources: Federal Reserve System, *Survey of Consumer Finances, 1983, 1989, 1992, 1995, 1998, 2001.*

Nope! I won't subject you to another figure, but the percentage of families who are more than two months late making their debt payments has shown virtually no change for over a decade.[7]

And what are families doing with all this debt—spending it on frivolous and unneeded "feel-good" items? Again—wrong! In 2001, over 70% of family debt was for the biggest investment most families will make—a home—and this was up from 53% in 1989.[8] Also, the percentage of consumer debt used for buying vehicles was actually lower in 2001 than in 1989.[9]

Now, what about family savings? I've already presented evidence that the value of family investments (which is where money targeted for savings goes) has been rising—look back at Figure 18.

But how can the increasing net worth of families be consistent with reports of a declining savings rate by families? The answer is simple: The so-called personal savings rate numbers are misleading! They only measure part of family saving. Saving occurs in two ways. It occurs when families don't spend money and invest those funds in stocks, bonds, certificates of deposit, money market funds and accounts, homes, and other kinds of investments. But saving also occurs when assets like stocks, bonds, homes, and other property increase in value. Such increases in value are called "capital gains" in investment lingo.

When these capital gains are added to the money people are putting in savings and investment accounts, the savings picture looks much different and much brighter. The family savings rate is consistently between 10% and 12% of family income.[10] And the rate is closer to 20% if the money families contribute to the Social Security system is considered as savings.[11]

This positive financial picture bodes well for future retirees. Both the Congressional Budget Office, the official financial watchdog of Congress, and the American Association of Retired Persons (AARP), the largest association of retirees in the country, report the "baby boom" generation is in better financial shape for retirement than previous generations and will be the wealthiest retired generation in history.[12]

Smart Economics knows the right way to measure a family's debt burden is to look at either family net worth (investments minus debt) or the percentage of family income taken by debt payments. Both measures show no recent danger signs except in two cases: less-educated families for net worth and low-income families for debt load. At the same time, when family saving is correctly measured to include "capital gains" on homes, stocks, and other investments, the overall savings rate has not declined.

44 Do Women Earn Less Than Men?

Most Americans, rightfully so, are sensitive to discrimination. Discrimination occurs when two people, with the *same characteristics* except for race, sex, creed, or sexual orientation, are treated differently in the business world.

Much progress has been made to reduce discrimination in our country. But one place where it allegedly still exists is in the workplace for women. This is illustrated by the statistic showing the average female worker earned only 78% of what the average male worker made in 2002.[1] Although this is better than working women in 1960, who earned only 60% of working men, it's still a gap—and some say, discrimination—nevertheless.[2]

Some of you may be thinking, "Gotcha!" Numbers don't lie, and obviously the numbers show women earning less than men.

Well, not so fast. Notice the two words I have in italics in the definition of discrimination: *same characteristics*. For discrimination to occur, the individuals being compared must have the same characteristics except for the factor on which the discrimination is supposedly based—in this case, gender.

The problem with the 78% statistic is that it combines all women and their earnings and compares the result to all men combined and their earnings. It doesn't account for the fact that men and women *differ* by a whole bunch of characteristics that have fundamental impacts on earnings.

For example, if men tend to have more education, more experience, and take less time away from work than women, then we would expect their average earnings to be higher than women's. Also, if a greater percentage of men are in higher-paying occupations, like doctors, lawyers, engineers, and computer scientists, and a greater proportion of women are in lower-paying jobs, like clerks, waitresses, and retail salespersons, then men's incomes will be greater than women's.

So the 78% statistic is really meaningless because it doesn't compare just apples to oranges; it compares apples to oranges, lemons, limes, carrots, peas, and lettuce.

To determine if women are discriminated against in pay, the pay of men and women must be compared after carefully accounting for all the economic fundamentals that determine what someone is paid, including education, field of study or training, age, experience, full- or part-time work, time away from work, where the worker lives (the cost of living varies by region), fringe benefits, occupation, and industry.

When this is done, the pay gap between men and women dramatically declines. Some studies show the gap shrinking to as low as 2.5%.[3] Factors "hurting" women in their pay are their lesser work experience, greater part-time work, and more time away from work for childbearing and child care.

A very revealing study looked at the earnings of female and male college graduates. When middle-aged (ages thirty-five to forty-four) female and male college grads were compared with the same degree, field of study, and occupation, the results were startling. In thirty of the forty-nine categories, women's earnings were 90% or more of men's earnings, and in five of the categories, women's earnings were greater than 100% of men's earnings. There's also evidence that the gender pay gap is smaller for younger workers than for older ones.[4]

Studies also show that men and women are being promoted at the same rate. A survey of workers promoted in 1996 revealed that 25.4% of men and 26% of women had been promoted. And the factors associated with promotion were essentially the same for men and women, with job performance, self-requests for promotion, and company reorganization being the top three reasons for promotion for both genders.[5]

The key change for women in recent decades has been their increased access to fields and careers previously dominated by men. As their ability to enter these fields has expanded, women have enjoyed substantial boosts to their average earnings.

One dilemma for women, however, is their continuing role as primary caregivers for children. Far from being a cliché, balancing home and work is the biggest challenge for many women in seeking equality of pay with men.[6]

Smart Economics knows that comparing the pay of men and women is much more complicated than looking at the average earnings of all female and male workers. Before any conclusions are made, differences between men and women in education, training, experience, time at work, occupation, and industry—at a minimum—must be recognized and accounted for in the comparisons. Studies that do this find the pay gap is much smaller than popularly reported. In fact, in a majority of occupations requiring a college education, the pay gap has virtually disappeared.

45 Are the Rich Getting Richer and Everyone Else Getting Poorer?

You've heard the old adage, The rich are getting richer and the poor are getting poorer. Most of us don't think of ourselves as rich, and let's face it, we often like to feel sorry for ourselves. So thinking rich people are grabbing all the money can help justify why we don't have as much as we'd like.

Academics have a fancy phrase for comparing changes in the income earned by the rich and nonrich: "income inequality." Their recent writings about income inequality reveal a common theme: Income inequality is increasing. Or saying the same thing, the distribution of income is becoming more unequal among households. Some politicians have picked up on this result by claiming there are "two Americas," one for the rich and one for everyone else.

Support for the idea of increasing income inequality goes something like this. Take all American households and divide them into five parts according to income: the richest fifth, the next richest fifth, the middle income fifth, the next fifth of households in terms of income, and finally the poorest fifth of households.

From 1974 to 2003, the share of the total income pie earned by the richest fifth of households increased from 43% to 50%, whereas the share earned by the poorest fifth of households dropped from 4.5% to 3.4%.[1] In other words, the gap between the richest and poorest households widened.

Further, income watchers say, this is a reversal of a previous trend of the income gap between the rich and the poor shrinking. They claim the income gap actually narrowed from the early 1900s through the 1960s.[2]

When the average person hears or reads about rising income inequality—that is, a growing gap between the rich and poor—what does she or he think? Well, the person thinks the old adage is at work: The rich have gotten richer and the poor have gotten poorer.

But there could be another explanation. It could be that both the rich and the poor have gotten richer, but just that the rich have gotten richer at a faster rate. That is, both the rich and poor are getting a bigger slice of income pie, but the rich man's slice may be 20% bigger, while the poor man's slice is only 10% larger.

This alternative explanation appears to best fit the numbers. First look at Figure 21. It shows the percentage of households in five different income ranges. Importantly, the dollars of the income ranges are comparable each year in their purchasing power.

What is apparent is that households have moved up the income ladder. The percentages of households in the upper-income ranges (>$100,000 and $50,000–$100,000) have increased, whereas the percentages of households in the lower-income ranges have decreased. For example, in 1967, 14% of households earned less than $10,000, and only 3% of households earned more than $100,000. In 2003, 9% of households earned under $10,000, but 15% of households earned more than $100,000. Again, the purchasing power of the dollars in both years has been adjusted to be the same.

FIGURE 21. Percentage of Households by Income Range (2003$)

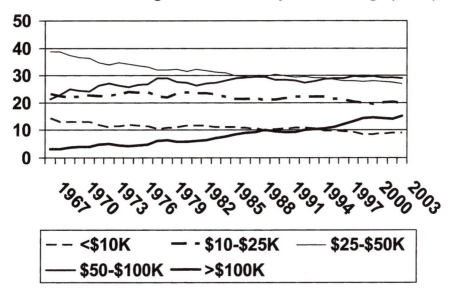

Source: U.S. Bureau of the Census, *Income, Poverty, and Health Insurance Coverage in the United States, 2003,* Table A-1.

FIGURE 22. Average Income of Household Income Groups (2003$)

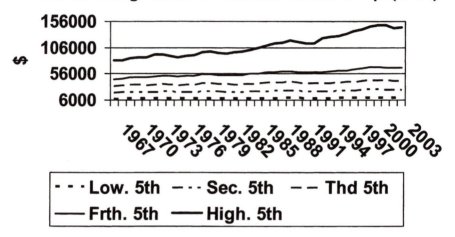

Source: U.S. Bureau of the Census, *Income, Poverty, and Health Insurance Coverage in the United States, 2003*, Table A-3.

Also look at Figure 22. It shows the average income in the five group-ings of households by income. The trend of each household income group is the same: up! The rich, and every other income group, got richer.

However, Figure 22 does show the richest group (high fifth) got richer faster than the other groups. Indeed, from 1967 to 2003, average income of the top fifth income group increased 76%, whereas average income of the other groups increased between 26% and 49%.[3]

Yet the statistics are really rigged to give this result. How so? It's be-cause the top income category (high fifth) has no ceiling, whereas the other income categories do. So as incomes generally rise, income in the top 20% of households will automatically grow faster than income in the other categories.[4]

There's another factor at work. One of the biggest determinants of in-come is education. Workers with more education earn more. And with the "tech revolution" of recent decades, the value of education, skills, and knowledge has become even greater. This means the bump-up in income from education has gotten bigger. So if the richest income category con-tains the greatest proportion of highly educated workers, average income in the richest category will increase faster than for the other income groupings.

Smart Economics reveals incomes of all income categories have moved higher in recent decades. Although the richest income category gained the most, this is mostly a result of the economy's greater value put on educated workers.

Is Poverty Getting Worse?

Turn on the evening news, especially during the Thanksgiving and Christmas holidays, and inevitably you'll see stories about homelessness, soup kitchens, and families "down on their luck," economically speaking. Poverty stories "play" because they are human interest, and they emit an emotional response from viewers.

Don't get me wrong—I feel sorry for families living in poverty. Through my federal taxes and private charitable contributions, I and all other taxpayers support programs to assist those living in poverty (see Chapter 5).

Yet the fact is, we have always had some families living in poverty, and we likely always will. But are we making any progress against poverty? By watching the stories on the evening news, it's easy to get the impression we're not. And indeed, the official statistics show the percentage of people living below the poverty line was higher in 2003 at 12.5% than in 1973, when it was 11.1%.[1]

However, one big problem with the overall poverty numbers is that they mask shifts in population groups that can have very different poverty rates and lead to "apples versus oranges" comparisons. Two of these shifts have had big impacts on the recent poverty statistics.

One is the dramatic increase in the Hispanic population, much of it from immigration. Compared to earlier immigrants, recent immigration has been composed of many more poor families.[2] So as increased immigration has pumped more poor families into the country at faster rates than the growth in the nonimmigrant population, the overall poverty rate is pushed up.[3]

The other is the relative increase in female-headed families—that is, families with no male present. The incidence of poverty is much higher in these families. In the past twenty years, families with children headed only by a female have grown at twice the rate as other families.[4]

A way to handle these shifts is to look at trends in poverty rates for households grouped by racial background and family composition. Figures 23, 24, and 25 do this and thus give "apples to apples" and "oranges to oranges" comparisons of poverty rates. Figure 23 shows trends in poverty rates for families headed by two parents, Figure 24 has the trends for female-headed families, and Figure 25 depicts the trends for single individuals (technically called "unrelated" individuals). Each figure has separate trends for whites, African Americans, and Hispanics.

All the figures show the poverty rates certainly have not gotten worse in recent decades, and actually, the rates improved—dropped—during the strong economic growth of the 1990s. For two-parent families, poverty rates are lowest for whites, followed by African Americans and then Hispanics. For female-headed families and unrelated individuals, poverty rates are again lowest for whites and then neck and neck for African Americans and Hispanics.

The numbers in the figures are the official figures from the U.S. Bureau of the Census. But even the Census Bureau admits their calculations may be too high. The official poverty measures are based on the money income earned by families. But the measures don't include the value of nonmoney benefits many low-income families receive, like Food Stamps, rent vouchers, and the large medical assistance programs Medicaid and Medicare.

FIGURE 23. Poverty Rates for Two-Parent Families

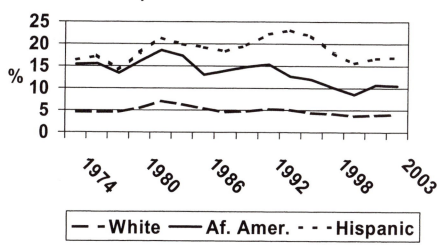

Source: U.S. Bureau of the Census, *Income, Poverty, and Health Insurance Coverage in the United States, 2003,* Table B-1.

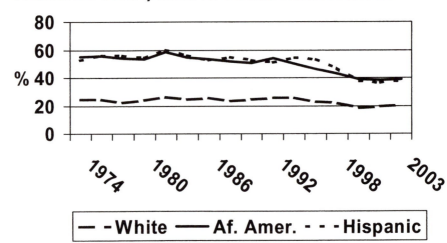

FIGURE 24. Poverty Rates for Female-Headed Families

Source: U.S. Bureau of the Census, *Income, Poverty, and Health Insurance Coverage in the United States, 2003*, Table B-1.

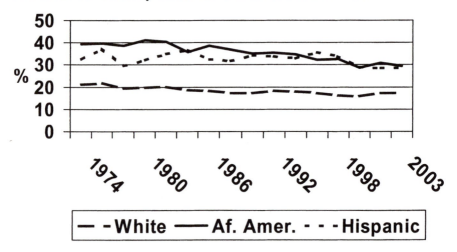

FIGURE 25. Poverty Rates for Unrelated Individuals

Source: U.S. Bureau of the Census, *Income, Poverty, and Health Insurance Coverage in the United States, 2003*, Table B-1.

When the value of nonmoney benefits are included, poverty rates are reduced by about one-third.[5] However, the pattern of poverty rates shown in Figures 23, 24, and 25 remains the same.

An alternative way of measuring poverty looks at what families *consume* rather than what they earn. By this measure, a tremendous reduction in poverty has occurred. Poor households in the 1990s owned, or had access to, more appliances, audiovisual equipment, and vehicles than did the average household in the early 1970s.[6]

Smart Economics goes behind the headlines to find that poverty rates have trended downward for all major household and racial groups, especially in the 1990s. When the noncash benefits received by low-income households are included, or when their consumption of products is examined, poverty rates are even lower than the official measures.

47 If It Saves One Life, Is It Worth the Cost?

You've had a long day and finally sit down to watch a little TV. On comes an interview program, and Senator Bigheart is answering questions from the host. "Senator Bigheart," says the host, "you've just sponsored a bill to spend $10 billion nationwide building reinforced concrete walls around public garbage dumpsters to prevent them from tipping over in high winds. There are only two recorded cases of anyone being injured from an over-turned dumpster. Would this be a wise use of public money?"

Senator Bigheart looks appalled, stares seriously into the camera, and states: "If it saves one life, it will be worth the expenditure." The audience breaks into applause, while the host says, "Of course, you're right, Senator Bigheart. Lives are much more important than money."

At a philosophical level, Senator Bigheart is right. But at a practical level, the senator is wrong. Before you accuse me of being insensitive, uncaring, and twisted, let me submit that the evidence supporting my position comes directly from *you*. The actions of each of us in our everyday lives tell me that people do set limits in what they will do and spend to save a life or prevent an injury—even if the life in question is their own.

How many of you buy a $100,000 armored vehicle for your day-to-day commuting, even though an armored car would give you the best pro-tection in case of a crash? How many of you live in a $300,000 steel and concrete home that is more fire resistant than a $100,000 frame home? Or how many of you hire round-the-clock security guards for protection rather than relying on the family dog?

I'll bet few of you answered "I do" to the above questions, and the rea-sons why are easy to understand. Even though each of these expenditures would add to your family's safety and protection, there are other demands on your money that are more important. You settle for a $200,000 wood frame home that could burn, instead of a $300,000 concrete and steel house, because that frees up $100,000 to spend in the future on food, clothing, your child's college education, and vacations. The same goes for the armored vehicle and round-the-clock security guard.

There are always many competing uses for our money. And although safety and security are important, they are not always primary. Spending $1,000 more on safety means $1,000 less is available to spend on gas, electricity, car repairs, or whatever you or your family needs.

All of us face these choices (even Bill Gates and Donald Trump have many alternative uses for their money), but we all don't make the *same* choices. Some families will sacrifice eating out, a larger home, and vacations to spend more on security and protection. Each family will weigh the pluses and minuses of different uses of their money and come to conclusions about what is right for *them*. One of the nice things about our country and economy is that families are free to do just this.

Sure, the government will put some restrictions on how we spend our money and what we do. Seatbelts and airbags are good examples. But whenever there are proposals for government-imposed safety mandates that result in consumers paying more for products, there is a big, big debate. Some groups, rightly so, will point out the private costs of these mandates, including what consumers *won't* be able to buy if they must spend more on vehicles with airbags. Then these costs must be weighed against the benefits of the mandates in terms of saved lives and reduced injuries. This is exactly the kind of comparison that should take place around the government conference table, just as it takes place around the household kitchen table.

Doesn't Senator Bigheart know all this? Doesn't Senator Bigheart know that spending $10 billion to save, say, two lives is unwise (I'm being polite) in light of the fact that the $10 billion could probably be spent in scores of other ways, both public and private, that would save more lives? Sure, Senator Bigheart probably knows this.

But there's a big difference between the decisions of Senator Bigheart and those of families. Familes are making choices about their *own* money, and they know that spending money in one way means it can't be spent in other ways. Senator Bigheart is making choices about spending *other people's money*, so, quite frankly, Senator Bigheart focuses on the benefits and conveniently ignores the costs.

In fact, it's unlikely in Senator Bigheart's $10 billion proposal any mention will be made of where the funds would come from. This is easy to do within a total federal budget of over $2 trillion. Of course, ultimately, the $10 billion would have to come either from new taxes, new borrowing (which just implies future taxes), or reductions in other programs. If pressed on this question, Senator Bigheart would probably say, "Surely, in this rich country, we can find money to save lives." The host wipes away a tear.

The point is this. One of the reasons economics is called the "dismal science" is that economics forces us to recognize nothing is free. At any point in time, you, me, businesses, and the government only have so many resources. If we increase spending on one thing, we have to decrease spending on something else. So ultimately choices about spending come down to comparing alternative benefits. So do I benefit more by spending $1,000 on X or on Y?

This reality can get blurred when our lives are at stake, but even then people do analyze trade-offs. After the World Trade Center attacks on 9/11, air travel did decrease, but it didn't stop. Although people perceived a greater risk to flying, many continued to fly because they put a greater value on the benefits of quicker trips, or they realized there were bigger risks to other forms of travel (i.e., auto travel is riskier, per mile driven, than air travel).

Although this may sound coldhearted, there are limits to what we will spend for safety and security. We do it every day. Our brains are constantly doing a balancing, and rebalancing, of our resources to give us the greatest net benefits. We want elected officials to do the same.

Smart Economics knows two fundamental realities: At any point in time, we have limited resources, and increasing spending on one outcome therefore implies decreasing spending on another outcome. So in considering spending to save lives and reduce injuries, we must weigh this spending in its effectiveness as well as in its implications for *reduced* spending on other things that affect our well-being. Households implicitly do this everyday. We should hold politicians to the same standard.

48 Can Families Afford College?

Beginning as early as elementary school, students have it drilled into them that they must go to college to get a good-paying job. Sure, there are always exceptions to every rule, and millionaires can be found today who are high school dropouts. But for the average person, a college degree is the ticket to prosperity.

Recognizing the importance of a college education, college students receive a tremendous amount of help. Only 18% of the revenues to public universities and colleges come from student tuition and fees.[1] The biggest single source of income for public higher education institutions is state appropriations.[2] Translated, this means state taxpayers are picking up the biggest part of the tab for public colleges.

Yet the 18% of college revenues paid by students is up from 13% twenty years ago.[3] Annual tuition and fees at public four-year colleges have jumped 143%, in inflation-adjusted terms, between 1976 and 2003, over six times faster than the increase in median household income.[4] As a result, yearly public college tuition and fee costs as a percentage of median household income rose from 5.3% in 1976 to 10.5% in 2003.

So despite the substantial help college students receive from taxpayers and other sources, college costs charged to students and their families have increased, thereby apparently making college less affordable. How does this make sense when a college education has become more important? Won't these increased costs cause some students not to attend college?

There are two responses to these important questions. First, all of the above calculations ignore college financial aid that doesn't have to be repaid in the form of outright grants as well as tax breaks. Those grants and tax breaks have increased substantially in recent years, and as a result, one study found that once the financial aid is accounted for, the average tuition at public universities actually paid by students dropped by almost one-third between 1998 and 2003.[5]

It's similar to comparing the sticker price of a car and the price actually paid after incentives. The sticker price (published tuition cost) can go up, while the price actually paid by the buyer, after incentives, goes down. This is exactly what has happened recently with college costs.

But even if financial aid is ignored, college costs can still be affordable if they're compared to the financial *benefits* of a college degree. Whenever we buy anything, we make a comparison of the benefits from the product compared to its costs. Hungry for lunch? You may consider the benefits of a Big Mac (taste, nutrition, shutting down the hunger pains) compared to its cost. If the benefits are greater than the costs, you'll probably buy!

And if, for some reason, the perceived benefits from eating Big Macs increase (maybe someone will find Big Macs actually cause weight *loss*), then you'd be willing to pay more for the tasty double-deckers.

Although I don't want to imply a college education is like a Big Mac, the situation I've described above directly applies to getting a college degree. Sure, the cost of four years of tuition and fees at public colleges rose from $7,359 to $18,776 between 1977 and 2003.[6] But the extra lifetime income earned by a college graduate compared to a high school graduate *increased* by over $130,000 over the same time period.[7]

So despite the higher costs to students, college is still a good financial deal for the average student, and in fact, the deal has actually gotten sweeter over the past three decades. Yes, students are paying more, but they're getting much, much more back. Figure 26 shows the increase in four-year tuition and fee costs from 1977 to 2003 compared to the increase in lifetime income of college graduates over the same time period.

So what's the problem? For many students and their families, the problem is they just can't come up with the money for tuition, even though they know these costs will be repaid many times over with the extra income earned by having the college degree. Maybe they started saving for college too late, or maybe they just couldn't find the money to save with all their other spending demands. And even if they qualify for financial aid or loans, they still may not be able to pay the remaining costs.

Perhaps what is needed is a radical new way of paying for college, a idea that may increase access to college while at the same time establishing a permanent revenue source for college funding.

FIGURE 26. Gains from a College Degree Have Far Exceeded the Costs

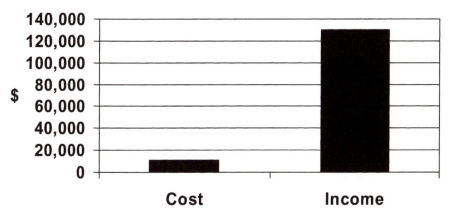

The idea is first based on the notion that state taxpayers benefit from a college-educated workforce, because such a workforce attracts higher-paying jobs, and holders of these jobs pay more in taxes and use less public assistance. So just as they do now, state taxpayers would continue to share in the costs of higher education.

But the plan is secondly based on the obvious fact that individual students directly benefit from a college education by earning substantially more income over their lifetime.

A way to combine these two points is this. Students would attend state-supported public colleges and universities tuition free. Yes, while in school, students would pay no tuition and fees. Students would, however, continue to pay room and board, for the simple reason that these costs aren't directly related to college. If the individual wasn't in college, he or she would still have to live somewhere and eat, so room and board costs would continue.

Also, there would need to be some limits on the amount of time students were in college. Perhaps if they weren't finished after five years, their tuition-free ride would end.

Here's the unique part of the plan. Once students graduated from college and were working, they would be required to repay a percentage of their tuition and fee costs—maybe 50% of the costs—from the increased earnings they derive by having a college degree. Policymakers could vary the percentage repaid with the earnings level of the student, and the repayment rate could be substantially higher for students who leave the state upon graduation.

Such a plan would have to be phased in over time, by gradually reducing tuition and fees while gradually increasing the payback of graduates. Yet it could offer a financially viable way to expand access to college while at the same time reducing the burden on state taxpayers.

Smart Economics observes that college costs charged to students have increased, yet recent increases in financial aid have softened the blow. However, the benefits to students of having a college degree have increased even more. So college is still an excellent financial deal for students. Changing the way that public colleges are financed, by having students pay tuition and fees from their increased earnings *after* they graduate, may be a solution whose time has come.

49 Would Importing Drugs Lower Their Prices?

Prescription drug prices have become a major issue for elderly households. Many of the elderly require prescription drugs, quite frankly, to stay alive or, at least, to lead an enjoyable life. Yet for many golden-year consumers, prescription drug prices appear to be going through the roof. In fact, since 1990, prescription drug prices have risen twice as fast as all other consumer prices.[1]

Some see a solution in importing drugs from other countries, most especially from Canada. Prescription drug prices, and indeed, prices of all medical services, are controlled by the Canadian government and are significantly lower than drug prices in the United States.[2] Lobbyists for the elderly see the answer to high drug prices as simply allowing purchases by U.S. consumers of drugs from Canada. Actually, despite legal questions about this practice, there is an active Internet market for doing just this.

Buying prescription drugs from Canada seems like a simple solution, but unfortunately for supporters of the idea, it's no solution at all for two big reasons. First, the Canadian market couldn't handle the demand. The Canadian pharmaceutical market is less than a tenth the size of the U.S. market.[3] There simply aren't enough prescription drugs in Canada to supply U.S. buyers.

And why not, you might ask, wouldn't pharmaceutical companies in Canada simply manufacture more drugs? Actually no, because Canada buys many of its prescription drugs from U.S. companies, and this leads to the second reason why the idea would fail: U.S. drug companies wouldn't let it happen.

Now I know this sounds conspiratorial and evil, but it really isn't. Here's what's going on. Currently, U.S. drug companies price prescription drugs differently for the Canadian and U.S. markets using a common business technique called *market segmentation*.[4] It's the same method airlines use to sell the same ticket to different customer groups, like business travelers and vacation travelers, at different prices.

The goal of market segmentation is to increase profits for the seller by dividing buyers into distinctive groups and selling to each group at different prices. One of the common characteristics for classifying buyers is income. Higher-income consumers are willing to pay more and so will be charged more than lower-income buyers. And guess what? Canadian households are poorer, on average, than U.S. households.[5] Therefore, U.S. drug companies have decided it's in their interest to charge American buyers more and Canadian buyers less for prescription drugs. Of course, this only works as long as the U.S. and Canadian markets are kept legally separate.

Then what would happen if there were no legal restrictions barring Americans from purchasing Canadian drugs? Well, despite the fact that the Canadian market couldn't handle the additional traffic, the drug companies would simply end their market segmentation. They would treat the U.S. and Canadian markets as one market. Canadian drug prices would rise, and U.S. drug prices would fall. But because the U.S. market is so much larger, the new price would be much closer to the old U.S. price, and savings to U.S. buyers would be small, perhaps as low as 1%.[6]

Aha, you may be thinking, if buying prescription drugs from Canada isn't the answer, then maybe the answer is to imitate the Canadians in another way—controlling prescription drug prices. Just have the U.S. government tell drug companies their prices can't go above a certain level, or have the government regulate how much drug prices can increase in any year. Problem solved!

But there will be a "bitter aftertaste" to this solution. Developing, testing, and ultimately receiving governmental approval to market new drugs is an extremely long and costly process. It costs an average of $800 million and takes twelve years to get a new drug to the market.[7] And once development of a new drug is begun, there's no assurance the company will make a dime from its efforts.

This means drug companies must recover the costs of developing both successful and unsuccessful drugs from the prices they charge. To encourage companies to take the very high risks and costs of trying to find new drugs, the government gives companies an initial monopoly over sale of their drugs for a twelve- to fifteen-year period.

The problem with government control of prescription drug prices is that politicians would have an incentive to keep the prices low. And the problem with this is that it might "kill the goose that lays the golden eggs." If drug companies can't charge prices high enough to recover their costs and give them an acceptable profit, they simply will stop developing new drugs. Indeed, it's no coincidence that the United States is home to most of the major drug research in the world, in no small part due to the fact that many other countries control prescription drug prices.[8]

So what are elderly users of prescription drugs supposed to do? Just grin and bear the escalating costs of prescription drugs? Actually yes, but with these caveats. Although prescription drug prices have recently risen faster than other prices, spending on prescription drugs still takes only 3.4% of elderly households' incomes, about the same as electricity.[9]

Also, increased consumption of prescription drugs contributed six times more to the total increase in cost than the increase in drug prices during the 1990s.[10] Translated: The big reason prescription drug costs to consumers have increased is that doctors are prescribing greater quantities of the drugs to patients.

The fact is that prescription drugs have become a more important part of medical treatments. We should be thankful for this because prescription drugs are making important contributions to the well-being of millions of people. Without prescription drugs, millions of Americans wouldn't be alive today or their existence would be much less pleasurable.

Also realize the prices of individual prescription drugs *drop* significantly once the monopoly provided to the drug company ends. This occurs as a result of competing *generic* drugs now being available in addition to the original name-brand drug. If numerous generic drugs are ultimately marketed, studies show the price can fall by as much as 90%.[11]

There is one practical tactic buyers of prescription drugs can use while the monopoly for a drug developer is in effect. This is to engage in collective buying. If buyers ban together into groups and use the power of group buying against the monopoly seller, significant price reductions can often be achieved.[12]

Smart Economics knows allowing Americans to legally buy prescription drugs from Canada is not the answer to high drug prices. The difference in prices between the United States and Canada would ultimately disappear, and the new prices would be very similar to the previous U.S. prices. The initial high price paid for prescription drugs is the motivation needed to encourage expensive and risky development of new drugs. However, when the drug developer's monopoly control lapses and generic substitutes are allowed, prices drop like a rock.

50 Can Government Lower Consumers' Health Costs?

In 2003, over $1.7 trillion was spent on health care in the United States.[1] This accounted for 15% of all spending in the country.[2] Both the dollar amount and, more important, the percentage rate are higher than for other industrialized countries.[3]

Some see this as a problem, and they say the source of the problem is the way health care is financed in our country. The U.S. health-care system is financed by a mix of private and public sources. Most working households have health insurance as a fringe benefit through their workplace. Elderly and low-income households have much of their health care paid by the federal government's two large medical programs, Medicare and Medicaid.

Critics say the U.S. system is complex and uncoordinated and leaves many households uninsured or underinsured. They also say the system wastes money in administrative costs.[4] And because health-care choices are largely driven by the decisions of consumers and doctors, critics say the U.S. system discourages less expensive preventative care and encourages more costly treatments once medical problems occur.

An oft-mentioned suggestion is for the United States to adopt a single-payer health-care system completely financed by the government. Canada and several European countries have the single-payer system. It's a system where the government pays everyone's health-care bills. Financing for the system comes from taxes.

So if you have a medical problem, under the single-payer system you go to a doctor or hospital and receive treatment, then the government pays the bill. What could be easier? And everyone in the country is covered, regardless of their work status or income, because taxes pay the bills.

On the surface, it looks like the single-payer system works. Everyone has health insurance. People don't have to worry about paying medical bills. Furthermore, countries with single-payer systems pay a lower percentage of their national income for health care than does the United States, so it looks like the single-payer system is more efficient and actually contains health-care costs.

But before you open the window and begin yelling, "Single-payer health care system now," let me deflate your enthusiasm with the "law of demand." The law of demand is not something your local city council or state legislature passed. Instead, the law of demand is a major tenant of economics that states a very simple observation: People use more of something, the lower its price.

Think about it. If the price of ground beef falls and nothing else changes, you'll likely buy more ground beef and less of substitutes for beef like pork, chicken, and fish. Similarly, if the price of gasoline falls, as it did in the 1990s, you'll probably drive more and maybe even buy a bigger, less-fuel-efficient vehicle like an SUV or pickup.

So what's the law of demand have to do with the single-payer health-care system? Well, in the single-payer system, the price of health care to the consumer is effectively *zero*. Although consumers ultimately pay the taxes financing the single-payer system, there's no *direct* relationship between the amount of health care by a person and taxes paid by that person. In short, the cost of health care is decoupled from the use of health care in the single-payer system. Indeed, this is exactly what the supporters of the single-payer system want.

But, going back to the law of demand, what will consumers do when the price of health care drops to zero? That's right, they'll use more health care. Well, duh, isn't this good? Isn't it good that the single-payer system motivates people to seek medical care more often when they're sick or suffer an injury?

Yes, that may be true, but the more medical care used, the greater the total cost of medical care. And the greater the total cost of medical care in the single-payer system, the more taxes that will have to be collected to support the system. And, of course, most people don't like paying higher taxes.

So unless politicians are willing to increase tax rates to fund more medical care, managers of the single-payer system face a problem. Without being able to increase the direct price of medical care to curtail use by consumers, managers have to find some other way to keep total costs under control.

They have found a tool to contain costs—waiting time. Statistics show that consumers wait longer for treatment in single-payer systems like Canada than in multipayer systems like the United States. For example, Canadians wait three times longer for some cancer treatments than patients in the United States.[5] Of course, during the wait, consumers can suffer, or the illness or injury may get worse. Canadians are also behind other countries in the availability of modern medical technology.[6]

So if a government-controlled single-payer system isn't the answer to controlling health-care costs, what is? The answer, in two words, is "increasing competition."

Four changes would inject more competition into the health-care system and cause it to give greater attention to consumers and to controlling costs.[7] First, have hospitals and doctors provide price and quality information to consumers so they can effectively shop among alternative providers.

Second, for those consumers needing financial assistance, directly subsidize them rather than providers. Paying providers to care for low-income or uninsured consumers encourages the providers to ignore costs. Subsidizing consumers to purchase their own private health insurance policies puts the consumer in control and also motivates consumers to more carefully consider costs.

Third, public decision makers should be cautious in mandating coverage for particular illnesses or treatments. Although such mandates may be well meaning and appear progressive, they will obviously add to health-care costs.

Fourth, state decision makers should reconsider their restrictions on increases in the supply of health-care facilities and technology. In the majority of states, hospitals aren't allowed to expand or purchase a new MRI (magnetic resonance imaging) machine, for example, without approval from the state. The federal government has determined that these restrictions, by limiting supply, have actually increased health-care prices to consumers, rather than controlling health costs as intended.[8]

Smart Economics knows the single-payer health-care system comes with its own costs. Since it's financed by general tax revenues, it appears to be "free" to users. Although "free" in money terms, it's not free in time. Because single-payer systems encourage more use of the medical system, the only way the system can control total costs is to ration care with time—that is, to make patients wait longer for treatment. So the single-payer system will provide free care—sometime!

A better approach is for government to enact reforms that increase competition among health-care providers. However, realize that as incomes and living standards rise, health-care expenditures will likely increase even more.[9]

Glossary

Average tax rate: taxes paid as a percentage of the taxpayer's income

Budget deficit: occurs when government expenditures exceed government revenues

Business incentives: public funds provided to a business, usually in the form of reductions in taxes or infrastructure improvements, in exchange for the business locating in a particular state or locality

Business productivity: a comparison of the amount of output produced by a business to the amount of inputs used in the production

Capital budget: a governmental budget related to long-lasting projects like roads, public buildings, equipment, and other infrastructure

Capital gains: earnings related to the increase in value of the underlying investment

Collusive oligopoly: occurs when a small number of businesses in the same industry agree to cooperative pricing and production policies

Comparative advantage: the motivation for international trade based on each country's specializing in what it does best.

Corporation: a form of business organization composed of investors, workers, and managers

Cost of living: a composite measure of the prices of products and services purchased by the typical consumer

Deflation: a consistent reduction in an average of prices

Demand: applies to the relationship between the amount of a product or service purchased by buyers and the price of the product or service

Direct taxes: taxes clearly identified as an individual category

Discretionary income: income remaining after spending on necessities and taxes

Discrimination: occurs when buyers or sellers are treated differently in economic transactions based on their inherent characteristics

Earned income tax credit: government payment to a low-income worker based on the worker's level of earnings

Energy self-sufficiency: occurs when a country produces all its energy resources and has no need to import energy resources from other countries

Entrepreneur: a businessperson seeking profit-making opportunities in new products, services, or technologies

Exchange rate: the rate at which the currency of one country trades for the currency of another country

Exports: the sale of products and services produced in a country to buyers in foreign countries

Federal Reserve: the central bank of the United States with powers over the growth in the nation's money supply and the level of short-term interest rates

Flat tax: a tax where the percentage of income or spending paid in the tax is the same for all taxpayers

Food Stamp Program: a government program that provides resources to low-income households for the purchase of food

Free trade: occurs when trade between countries is not impeded by barriers such as tariffs and quotas

Generic drugs: drugs sold without the label of the original manufacturer

Gold standard: the tying of a nation's money supply to the quantity of gold it owns

Government spending on services: government spending that produces a tangible product or activity, such as roads, educational facilities, and national security forces

Government spending on transfers: government spending that provides or supports financial resources for recipients

Gross income: income before adjustments for allowable tax deductions and exemptions

Imports: the purchase of products and services produced in foreign countries

Income inequality: measures the degree of income disparity between households

Income-tested programs: government programs available for households based on their level of income

Indirect taxes: taxes that are hidden in the price of a product or service

Industry: the collection of businesses producing the same product or service

Inflation: a consistent increase in an average of prices

Input: a resource used to produce a product or service

Insourcing: jobs created and economic activities conducted in a country by companies from foreign countries

Instructional spending: educational spending on activities in the classroom

Law of demand: the idea that purchases of a product or service increase when the price falls and decrease when the price rises

Leakage effects: local spending that leaves the area when it is spent on products and services produced outside the locality

Living wage: a wage rate high enough to provide some defined standard of living

Long-term interest rate: an interest rate on an investment with a lengthy investment period

Luxury goods: products or services whose purchases increase at a faster rate than the increase in the buyer's income

Marginal tax rate: the change in taxes paid as a percentage of the change in the taxpayer's income

Market segmentation: selling the same product or service to different buyer groups at different prices

Marriage tax bonus: occurs when a married couple pays less taxes than they would have as singles

Marriage tax penalty: occurs when a married couple pays more taxes than they would have as singles

Medicaid: the government program that pays a share of the health-care expenses of low-income households

Mercantilism: an economic philosophy that says a nation's prosperity is linked to increases in exports to foreign countries

Minimum wage: a government-mandated wage rate that businesses must at least pay

Monopoly: occurs when only one seller exists in an industry

Multiplier: a factor used to expand initial new spending in a region to obtain total new spending in a region after accounting for economic interrelationships

NAFTA: North American Free Trade Agreement; an agreement between the United States, Canada, and Mexico to reduce trade barriers between the countries

National debt: the total amount of borrowing by the federal government existing at a point in time

Negative income tax: a tax system in which taxpayers below established income levels receive new income from the Internal Revenue Service

Net worth: the difference between the value of an individual's assets and investments and his or her outstanding debt

Noncash benefits: governmental assistance in the form of services or products instead of money

Occupation: the specific tasks a person does in a job

Operating budget: public spending for daily functions of government agencies, including payroll, energy use, and travel

Opportunity cost: the foregone benefits of spending choices not selected

Output: the product or service produced from inputs

Outsourcing: jobs created and economic activities conducted in foreign countries by domestic companies

Personal exemptions: allowances based on the number of people in a household on which income tax is not paid

Personal savings rate: household income remaining after spending and after taxes and expressed as a percentage of household income

Price controls: occurs when government puts upper limits on the price of a product or service

Price gouging: refers to prices some believe are too high compared to the cost of the product or service and that provides the seller with an exceptionally high profit

Privatization: shifting functions and activities performed by government agencies to private businesses

Profit: monies to a business after all input costs and taxes are deducted

Progressive tax: a tax where the percentage of income paid increases as the taxpayer's income increases

Proportional tax: a tax where the percentage of income paid is the same for all levels of the taxpayer's income

Purchasing power: the quantity of products and services a dollar can buy at a particular point in time

Real interest rate: equals the observed interest rate minus the inflation rate

Real investment return: equals the earnings from an investment, expressed as a percentage, minus the inflation rate

Real price: when comparing price changes over time, equals the observed change in price adjusted for inflation over the same time period

Regressive tax: a tax where the percentage of income paid decreases as the taxpayer's income increases

Sales tax: a tax paid on the purchase of certain products or services

Service sector: all economic activity outside of manufacturing, construction, and farming

Shortage: occurs when buyers desire to purchase more of the product or service than producers want to sell at the stated price

Short-term interest rate: an interest rate on an investment with a relatively brief investment period

Single-payer system: a health-care system where all expenditures are paid by taxes collected by the government

Social Security surplus: excess Social Security taxes collected today in order to fund the pensions of future retirees

Social Security tax system: taxes collected from today's workers in order to fund the pensions of current and future retirees

Standard deduction: an amount taxpayers can use to reduce their taxable income instead of using itemized deductions

Strengthening dollar: occurs when the number of units of foreign currencies exchanged for one U.S. dollar increases

Supply: applies to the relationship between the amount of a product or service produced by businesses and the price of the product or service

Taxable income: income taxed after accounting for personal exemptions, deductions, and other adjustments

Tax bracket: a range of income to which a specific income tax rate applies

Tax burden: total taxes paid as a percentage of income

Tax credit: an approved expenditure that directly reduces the amount of taxes paid

Tax deduction: an approved expenditure that reduces taxable income

Tax write-off: a common name for a tax deduction

Trade deficit: occurs when a country imports more products and services from foreign countries than it exports to those countries

Trade surplus: occurs when a country exports more products and services to foreign countries than it imports from those countries

Transition issue: applies to temporary additional funding required for Social

Security if workers are permitted to direct some of their Social Security taxes to private accounts

Unit labor cost: the cost of a worker required to produce one unit of a product or service

U.S. government Treasury security: investments with the U.S. government used to fund budget deficits

Weakening dollar: occurs when the number of units of foreign currencies exchanged for one U.S. dollar decreases

WTO: World Trade Organization; an agreement among 147 countries to reduce trade barriers

■ Notes ■

Chapter 1: Has Government Growth Been Out of Control?

1. President's Council of Economic Advisors, *Economic Report of the President, 2004* (Washington, D.C.: U.S. Government Printing Office, 2004), Table B-82, http://www.gpoaccess.gov/eop/index.html.

2. The purchasing power adjustment was made using the all-items consumer price index, http://www.bls.gov.

3. Spending on services and transfers are for federal, state, and local governments combined and are defined by the U.S. Department of Commerce. See Council of Economic Advisors, *Economic Report of the President, 2004*, Table B-83.

Chapter 2: Will the National Debt Sink Our Economic Future?

1. Federal Reserve Bank of St. Louis, *National Economic Trends*, May 2004, http://www.research.stlouisfed.org.

2. Federal Reserve System, "Recent Changes in U.S. Family Finances: Evidence from the 1998 and 2001 Survey of Consumer Finances," *Federal Reserve Bulletin* 89, no. 1 (2003): 1–32.

3. Federal Reserve Bank of St. Louis, *National Economic Trends*. If state and local debt is included, total government debt in the United States as a percentage of national income is 75%. See Tax Foundation, *Facts and Figures on Government Finance, 37th Edition* (Washington, D.C.: Author, 2003), Table D1.

4. For example, the national debt to national income ratio in 2003 was 118% in Italy, 155% in Japan, and 70% in France and averaged 77% in the European Community countries. Federal Reserve Bank of St. Louis, *International Economic Trends*, May 2004, http://www.research.stlouisfed.org.

5. Federal Reserve Bank of St. Louis, *National Economic Trends,* April 2005, http://www.research.stlouisfed.org.

Chapter 3: Do Budget Deficits Increase Interest Rates?

1. See, for example, N. Gregory Mankiw, *Principles of Economics*, 2nd ed. (Orlando, Fla.: Harcourt College Publishers, 2001), 572.

2. Some examples are Paul Evans, "Interest Rates and Expected Future Budget Deficits in the United States," *Journal of Political Economy* 95, no. 1 (1987): 34–58; Evans, "Do Budget Deficits Raise Nominal Interest Rates? Evidence from Six Countries," *Journal of Monetary Economics* 20, no. 2 (1987): 281–300; Evans, "Is Ricardian Equivalence a Good Approximation?" *Economic Inquiry* 29, no. 4 (1991): 626–644; Robert Barro, "The Ricardian Approach to Budget Deficits," *Journal of Economic Perspectives* 3, no. 2 (1989): 37–54; and Roger Kormendi, "Government Debt, Government Spending, and Private Sector Behavior," *American Economic Review* 73, no. 5 (1983): 994–1010.

3. Professor John Seater has explored this theory in some detail. Some of his relevant publications include "Are Future Taxes Discounted?" *Journal of Money, Credit, and Banking* 14, no. 3 (1982): 376–389; "Does Government Debt Matter?: A Review," *Journal of Monetary Economics* 16, no. 1 (1985): 121–131; and "Ricardian Equivalence," *Journal of Economic Literature* 11, no. 2 (1993): 265–277. The theory was originally developed by David Ricardo, an eighteenth-century economist.

4. Some economists have found a positive link between *forecasts* of budget deficits and *forecasts* of interest rates. See Thomas Laubach, "New Evidence on the Interest Rate Effects of Budget Deficits and Debt" (working paper, Board of Governors of the Federal Reserve System, Washington, D.C., May 2003).

Chapter 4: Can Government Spending Be Cut by Eliminating Waste?

1. Economic Research Service, U.S. Department of Agriculture, http://www.ers.usda.gov.

2. President's Council of Economic Advisors, *Economic Report of the President, 2004*, Table B-100.

3. E. C. Pasour Jr., and Randal R. Rucker, *Agriculture and the State* (Oakland, Calif.: Independent Institute, 2001), Table 6.4.

4. Bruce L. Gardner, *American Agriculture in the Twentieth Century* (Cambridge, Mass.: Harvard University Press, 2002), Table 7.1.

Chapter 5: Does Government Spend Too Much, or Not Enough, on the Poor?

1. U.S. House Ways and Means Committee, *2004 Green Book* (Washington, D.C.: Government Printing Office, 2004), Appendix K, http://www.gpoaccess.gov/wmprints/green/2004/html.

2. The program spending amounts don't sum to $522 billion, owing to rounding. The major components are: medical—Medicaid; cash—supplemental security income and earned income tax credit; food—Food Stamps and school lunch program; housing—Section 8 housing assistance and low-rent public housing; education—Pell grants and Head Start; services—child care; job training—TANF (Temporary Assistance for Needy Families) work activities and job corps; and energy—low-income home energy assistance.

3. U.S. House Ways and Means Committee, *2004 Green Book*, Appendix H. In 2003, there were slightly more poor people, 35.9 million. See U.S. Census Bureau, *Income, Poverty, and Health Insurance Coverage in the United States, 2003*, Current Population Reports P60-226 (Washington, D.C.: Government Printing Office, August 2004), Table B-1. However, to be consistent with the dollar amounts for 2002, 2002 poverty numbers are used.

4. U.S. Census Bureau, *Poverty in the United States, 2002*, Current Population Reports P60-222 (Washington, D.C.: Government Printing Office, September 2003), Table A-1. In 2003, the number of poor households was 17.3 million. See U.S. Census Bureau, *Income, Poverty, and Health Insurance Coverage in the United States, 2003*.

5. A report by the government's financial watchdog, the U.S. Government Accounting Office, cited inherent incentives to overprovide services as a major factor in rising Medicaid costs. U.S. Government Accounting Office, *Medicare and Medicaid: Opportunities to Save Program Dollars by Reducing Fraud and Abuse* (Washington, D.C.: Government Printing Office, March 1995), http://www.gao.gov.

6. The selling of Food Stamps for cash is called trafficking. In the 1990s, the federal government estimated that 10% of Food Stamps were trafficked. U.S. Government Accounting Office, *Reducing Fraud and Abuse in the Food Stamp Program with Electronic Benefit Transfer Technologies* (Washington, D.C.: Government Printing Office, February 1994), http://www.gao.gov.

7. Milton Friedman, *Capitalism and Freedom* (Chicago: University of Chicago Press, 1962).

8. Edmund S. Phelps, *Rewarding Work* (Cambridge, Mass.: Harvard University Press, 1997).

Chapter 7: Does More Spent on Education Pay Off in Student Achievement?

1. U.S. Department of Education, National Center for Education Statistics, at http://nces.ed.gov/programs/digest/d02/tables/dt168.asp and http://nces.ed.gov/programs/digest/d02/tables/dt126.asp.

2. See E. Hanushek, "The Economics of Schooling: Production and Efficiency in the Public Schools," *Journal of Economic Literature* 24, no. 3 (1986): 1141–1177;

and Michael L. Walden and Mark S. Sisak, "School Inputs and Educational Out-comes in North Carolina: Comparison of Static and Dynamic Analyses," *Journal of Agricultural and Applied Economics* 31, no. 3 (1999): 593–609.

3. The results in Table 1 are based on an analysis by the author of 2000 year fourth-grade math scores from the National Assessment of Educational Progress, at http://nces.ed.gov/nationsreportcard/mathematics/results/stateavgscale-g4.asp. Spending amounts were from the U.S. Department of Education (see note 1 above) and were adjusted for differences in the cost of living in states using indices de-veloped by Walter W. McMahon: "Geographical Cost of Living Differences: An Update," *Journal of the American Real Estate and Urban Economics Association* 19, no. 3 (1991): 426–450. Rates of poverty and single-family headship were from the 2000 U.S. Census, http://www.census.gov. Over 71% of the variation in the state test scores was accounted for by the three factors.

4. U.S. Department of Education, National Center for Education Statistics, at http://nces.ed.gov/progress/digest/d02/tables/dt160.asp.

5. Walden and Sisak, "School Inputs and Educational Outcomes in North Car-olina."

6. One of the comprehensive studies has been in Tennessee. See Frederick Mosteller, "The Tennessee Study of Class Size," *The Future of Children* 5, no. 2 (1995): 113–127.

7. The argument that smaller class sizes can improve student academic perfor-mance is not without its critics. See Lawrence Mishel and Richard Rothstein, *The Class Size Debate* (Washington, D.C.: Economic Policy Institute, 2002).

8. Walden and Sisak, "School Inputs and Educational Outcomes in North Carolina."

Chapter 8: Has the Social Security Surplus Been Stolen?

1. Includes tax collections and interest earnings. Trustees of the Social Secu-rity System, *2005 Annual Report of the Board of Trustees of the Federal Old-Age, Sur-vivors, and Disability Insurance Trust Funds* (Washington, D.C.: Social Security Administration, 2005, Table III.A.1, http://www.ssa.gov/OACT/TR/TR04.

Chapter 9: Is Social Security Going Bankrupt?

1. Trustees of the Social Security System, *2005 Annual Report*, Figure II.D.7. Analysis by the Congressional Budget Office puts the bankruptcy date at slightly later, in 2052. Congressional Budget Office, *The Outlook for Social Security* (Wash-ington, D.C.: U.S. Government Printing Office, June 2004), Figure 1–2.

2. Technically, the Social Security Trustees only forecast Social Security's fu-ture for a maximum of seventy-five years. Some economists have criticized this

time horizon as being too short, and they have calculated bigger gaps for Social Security for longer time periods. Laurence Kotlikoff and Scott Burns, *The Coming Generational Storm* (Cambridge, Mass.: MIT Press, 2004).

3. Trustees of the Social Security System, *2005 Annual Report.*

4. Ibid., Table V.B1.

5. Alan Gustman and Thomas Steinmeirer, "How Effective Is Redistribution under the Social Security Benefit Formula?" (National Bureau of Economic Research working paper 7597, Cambridge, Mass., March 2000).

6. For greater discussion of the transition issue, see Peter Ferrara and Michael Tanner, *A New Deal for Social Security* (Washington, D.C.: The Cato Institute, 1998), Chapter 9; and Laurence Kotlikoff, "Privatizing U.S. Social Security: Some Possible Effects on Intergovernmental Equity and the Economy," *Review* (Federal Reserve Bank of St. Louis) 80, no. 2 (March–April 1998): 31–37.

7. An exception is Martin Feldstein and Andrew Samwick, "Potential Paths of Social Security Reform" (NBER working paper 8592, Cambridge, Mass., November 2001). Feldstein and Samwick argue privatizing Social Security will increase the funds available for business investment, and additional business investment will cause faster growth in the economy. They propose using some of the new income generated from this growth to finance the transition.

Chapter 10: Should Our Money Be Backed by Gold?

1. This is one reason why the Gold Commission in 1981 recommended against reestablishing the gold standard. *Report to the Congress of the Commission on the Role of Gold in the Domestic and International Monetary Systems* (Washington, D.C.: Government Printing Office, March 1982).

Chapter 11: Should Government Enforce a Living Wage?

1. Still one of the best analyses of the minimum wage is Joseph Stigler, "The Economics of Minimum Wage Legislation," *American Economic Review* 36, no. 3 (1946): 358–365. A more recent study of the minimum wage is in David Neumark and William Wascher, "The Effect of New Jersey's Minimum Wage Increase on Fast-Food Employment: A Reevaluation Using Payroll Records" (working paper no. 5224, National Bureau of Economic Research, Cambridge, Mass., August 1995); and Neumark and Wascher, "Minimum Wages, Labor Market Institutions, and Youth Employment: A Cross-National Analysis," *Industrial and Labor Relations Review* 57, no. 2 (2004): 223–248.

2. Steven Haugen, "Characteristics of Minimum Wage Workers in 2002," *Monthly Labor Review* 126, no. 9 (2003): 37–40.

3. Ralph Smith and Bruce Vavrichek, "The Wage Mobility of Minimum Wage Workers," *Industrial and Labor Relations Review* 45, no. 1 (1992): 82–88.

Chapter 12: Should Government Control the Prices of Necessities?

1. William Tucker, "How Rent Control Drives Out Affordable Housing" (Cato Policy Analysis No. 274, The Cato Institute, Washington, D.C., May 21, 1997).

2. Nadeem Esmail, *Waiting Your Turn: Hospital Waiting Lists in Canada* (Critical Issues Bulletin, The Fraser Institute, Vancouver, Canada, October 2003).

3. Jerry Taylor and Peter Van Doren, "California's Electricity Crisis: What's Going On, Who's to Blame, and What to Do?" (Cato Policy Analysis No. 406, The Cato Institute, Washington, D.C., July 3, 2001); and the Congressional Budget Office, *Causes and Lessons of the California Electricity Crisis* (Washington, D.C.: Government Printing Office, September 2001).

Chapter 13: Should Government Pay Businesses to Create Jobs?

1. Dennis A. Rondinelli and William J. Burpitt, "Do Government Incentives Attract and Retain International Investment? A Study of Foreign-Owned Firms in North Carolina," *Policy Sciences* 33, no. 1 (2000): 181–205.

2. Michael Greenstone and Enrico Moretti, "Bidding for Industrial Plants: Does Winning a 'Million Dollar Plant' Increase Welfare?" (working paper 9844, National Bureau of Economic Research, Cambridge, Mass., July 2003).

3. In 2000–2001, business incentives expenditures accounted for, at most, 1% of all state and local government spending. U.S. Bureau of the Census, http://www .census.gov/govs/www/estimate01.html.

Chapter 14: Can Government Create Prosperity?

1. Federal Reserve Bank of St. Louis, *National Economic Trends*.

2. George T. McCandless Jr. and Warren Weber, "Some Monetary Facts," *Quarterly Review* (Federal Reserve Bank of Minneapolis) 25, no. 4 (2001): 14–23.

Chapter 15: Do We Pay 60% to 80% of Our Income in Taxes?

1. President's Council of Economic Advisors, *Economic Report of the President, 2004*, Tables B-1, B-83.

2. Ibid.

3. Tax Foundation, "The Tax Burden of the Median American Family" (Special Report, No. 96, Washington, D.C., March 2000).

4. U.S. Bureau of Labor Statistics, *Consumer Expenditure Survey, 2002*, http://www.bls.gov. Total taxes include federal income taxes, all state and local taxes, and Social Security contributions. Similar results were found using slightly

different calculations by Don Fullerton and Diane Lim Rogers, *Who Bears the Lifetime Tax Burden?* (Washington, D.C.: Brookings Institution, 1993), 207.

5. Congressional Budget Office, *Effective Federal Tax Rates under Current Law, 2001 to 2014* (Washington, D.C.: Author, August 2004).

6. Laurence J. Kotlikoff, *Generational Accounting* (New York: Free Press, 1992).

Chapter 16: Does a Tax Bracket of 40% Mean the Government Takes 40% of Your Income?

1. Research Institute of America, *Federal Income Tax Handbook, 2005* (New York: Author, 2003), sections 3111, 3114. Assumes family uses the standard deduction.

2. The income ranges change each year, and the tax rates can change with new tax laws.

3. The tax rates on FICA can actually be lower for very high income households, compared to low-income taxpayers. The explanation for this is found in Chapter 22.

Chapter 17: Can Cutting Tax Rates Increase Tax Revenues?

1. Congressional Budget Office, *Projecting Federal Tax Revenues and the Effect of Changes in the Law* (Washington, D.C.: U.S. Government Printing Office, December 1998).

2. See Don Fullerton, "On the Possibility of an Inverse Relationship between Tax Rates and Government Revenues," *Journal of Public Economics* 19, no. 1 (1982): 3–22; Lawrence Lindsey, *The Growth Experiment* (New York: Basic Books, 1990); and Victor Canto, Douglas Joines, and Robert Webb, "The Revenue Effects of the Kennedy and Reagan Tax Cuts: Some Time Series Estimates," *Journal of Business and Economic Statistics* 40, no. 3 (1986): 281–287. Controversy does exist about whether reductions in tax rates applied to some investment returns, called capital gains taxes, can more than pay for themselves even though top capital gains tax rates are well below 50%. Studies have shown this can be the case over a few years as investors can time the sale of their investments to take advantage of the lower rates, but over a longer number of years, additional revenues do not pay for the tax cut. Congressional Budget Office, "Capital Gains Taxes and Federal Revenues," *Revenue and Tax Policy Brief*, October 9, 2002.

3. If state income tax payments are "deductible" for the federal income tax, then the combined rate would be 52% rather than 60% (40% + 20% − 20% × 0.4).

4. For the effects of cutting tax rates in one state or one city, see Michael L. Walden, "Dynamic Revenue Curves for North Carolina Taxes," *Public Budgeting and Finance* 23, no. 4 (2003): 49–64; and Robert P. Inman, "Can Philadelphia Escape Its Fiscal Crisis with Another Tax Increase?" *Business Review* (Federal Reserve Bank of Philadelphia) no. 5 (September–October 1992): 5–20.

Chapter 18: Will a Tax Cut of $1 Create $7 to $10 of New Income?

1. IMPLAN, Mig, Inc., Stillwater, Minn.

Chapter 19: Do Corporations Pay Too Little in Taxes?

1. Council of Economic Advisors, *Economic Report of the President, 2004*, Table B-80.
2. Congressional Budget Office, *The Incidence of the Corporate Income Tax* (Washington, D.C.: U.S. Government Printing Office, March 1996).

Chapter 20: Would Rich Investors Benefit from a Flat Tax?

1. For a comprehensive description of the flat income tax idea, see Robert E. Hall and Alvin Rabushka, *The Flat Tax*, 2nd ed. (Stanford, Calif.: Hoover Institution Press, 1995).
2. Mankiw, *Principles of Economics*, 805.

Chapter 21: Is the Sales Tax Regressive?

1. Fullerton and Rogers, *Who Bears the Lifetime Tax Burden?*
2. Ibid.

Chapter 22: Do the Rich Get a Break on Social Security Taxes?

1. Research Institute of America, *Federal Income Tax Handbook, 2005*, section 1107. The values are for 2005. The tax quoted is for an employee. A similar tax is paid by the employer. Self-employed workers pay both taxes. The income limit on which the tax is applied ($90,000 in 2005) is increased by the inflation rate each year.
2. http://www.socialsecurtiy.gov/OACT/ProgData/retirebenefit2.html. The dollar amounts increase with the inflation rate each year.

Chapter 23: Has the Tax Penalty for Marriage Been Ended?

1. Congressional Budget Office, *For Better or Worse: Marriage and the Federal Income Tax* (Washington, D.C.: U.S. Government Printing Office, June 1997).
2. Ibid.

Chapter 24: Is American Manufacturing Dying?

1. President's Council of Economic Advisors, *Economic Report of the President, 2004*, Table B-46.

2. Ibid., Table B-53.

3. Ibid., Tables B-46, B-51.

4. Ibid., Table B-100.

5. Ibid., Table B-99.

6. Ibid., Tables B-99, B-100. Comparisons are for 1999 and 1948.

7. Jon E. Hilsenrath and Rebecca Buckman, "Factory Employment Is Falling Worldwide," *Wall Street Journal*, October 20, 2003, A2.

Chapter 25: Are Low-Paying Jobs Replacing High-Paying Ones?

1. President's Council of Economic Advisors, *Economic Report of the President, 2004*, Table B-46.

2. This time period spans both years when the overall economy was improving as well as years when it was in recession.

3. U.S. Department of Commerce, Bureau of Economic Analysis, http://www.bea.doc.gov.

4. David E. Hecker, "Occupational Employment Projections to 2012," *Monthly Labor Review* 127, no. 2 (2004): 80–105.

Chapter 26: Are Companies Outsourcing Good-Paying Jobs?

1. Ed Frauenheim, "IBM Escalates Outsourcing to India and China," December 17, 2003, http://uk.builder.com/manage/business/0,39026582, 39118596.00.htm.

2. Charles L. Schultze, "Offshoring, Import Substitution, and the Jobless Recovery" (Brookings Institute, Policy Brief no. 136, Washington, D.C., August 2004).

3. Global Insight, "The Comprehensive Impact of Offshore IT Software on the U.S. Economy and the IT Industry" (company bulletin), Lexington, Mass., March 2004.

4. U.S. Department of Commerce. See note 3 in Chapter 25.

5. The increases were 35% for outsourcing and 31% for insourcing.

6. U.S. Department of Commerce. See note 3 in Chapter 25.

7. For 2001, 9,775,600 outsourced jobs minus 6,371,900 insourced jobs, with the result (3,403,700) taken as a percentage of total U.S. jobs of 131,826,000.

Chapter 27: Will Free Trade Destroy Our Economy?

1. The U.S. growth rate in the production of goods and services was 25.5% from 1995 to 2002. Council of Economic Advisors, *Economic Report of the President, 2004*, Table B-2.

2. Organization for Economic and Cooperative Development (OECD), at

http://cs4-hq.oecd.org/oecd/selected_view.asp?tableid=561&viewname=ana part31970.

3. Calculations based on wages and salaries and jobs per dollar of output in each industry category using data from the U.S. Department of Commerce.

4. Savings derived by applying the additional price consumers would have paid in 2003 for clothes, toys, and furniture if pre-1994 price trends had continued to purchases of these products in 2003, using data from the consumer price index and Consumer Expenditure Survey (http://www.bls.gov).

5. Savings calculated as the additional spending on imports if import prices rose like U.S. prices. The $140 billion is in inflation-adjusted 2002 dollars. Data are from the U.S. Department of Commerce.

6. From 1995 to 2002, only $188 million had been spent each year assisting an average of 32,000 workers who were displaced from their jobs owing to trade pacts. The average weekly payment per recipient was $206. U.S. House Ways and Means Committee, *2004 Green Book*, Table 6-3.

7. See note 4 in this chapter for procedure used to calculate the $20 billion savings.

8. Calculated as $10 billion divided by the number of textile and apparel job losses from 1995 to 2003 (798,000).

Chapter 28: Can U.S. Workers Compete with Low-Paid Foreign Workers?

1. Data are for 2001, U.S. Bureau of Labor Statistics, Foreign Labor Statistics, ftp://ftp.bls.gov/pub/special.requests/ForeignLabor/industry.txt.

2. William W. Lewis, *The Power of Productivity* (Chicago: University of Chicago Press, 2004).

3. U.S. Bureau of Labor Statistics, "International Comparisons of Manufacturing Productivity and Unit Labor Cost Trends, Revised Data for 2002," http://www.bls.gov.news.release/pdf/prod4.pdf.

Chapter 29: Do Countries Prosper Only If They Run a Trade Surplus?

1. U.S. Department of Commerce, Bureau of Economic Analysis. See note 3 in Chapter 25.

2. Federal Reserve Bank of St. Louis, *National Economic Trends*, June 2004, http://www.research.stlouisfed.org.

3. David W. Pearce, *The Dictionary of Modern Economics* (Cambridge, Mass.: MIT Press, 1981), 279.

4. The comparison does not account for any security or defense costs to the

United States of protecting the supplies of Middle East oil. See Chapter 39, "Should We Become Energy Self-Sufficient?"

5. In 2003, the trade deficit was $497 billion, while net foreign investment in the United States was $545 billion.

6. Foreign ownership of land is from "Foreign Ownership of U.S. Agricultural Land," U.S. Department of Agriculture, *AREI Updates*, #13, October 1996; foreign ownership of other assets is from Board of Governors of the Federal Reserve System, *Flow of Funds Accounts of the United States, 1995–2003* (Washington, D.C.: U.S. Department of Agriculture, June 10, 2004), Tables B100, B102, B103, and L107.

Chapter 32: Does Business Make Obscene Profits?

1. Corporate net income divided by corporate total receipts in 2000, from the Internal Revenue Service (http://www.irs.gov). Similar results are found for corporate profits as a percentage of national income (http://www.bea.doc.gov).

2. Internal Revenue Service. See note 1 above.

Chapter 33: Does Big Business Control the Economy?

1. See Lawrence J. White, "Trends in Aggregate Concentration in the United States," *Journal of Economic Perspectives* 16, no. 4 (2002): 137–160; and Joel Popkin and Company, *Small Business Share of Economic Growth* (Final Report to the U.S. Small Business Administration, Washington, D.C., December 14, 2001). Pryor finds modest increases in "big business" control in the 1990s. See Frederic L. Pryor, "News from the Monopoly Front: Changes in Industrial Concentration, 1992–1997," *Review of Industrial Organization* 20, no. 2 (2002): 183–185.

Chapter 34: Can Pro Sports Teams and Facilities Hit Economic Home Runs?

1. For examples of such studies and their critics, see Roger G. Noll and Andrew Zimbalist, *Sports, Jobs, and Taxes* (Washington, D.C.: Brookings Institution Press, 1997); Mark Rosentraub, *Major League Losers* (New York: Basic Books, 1997); and John Siegfried and Andrew Zimbalist, "The Economics of Sports Facilities and Their Communities," *Journal of Economic Perspectives* 14, no. 3 (2000): 95–114.

2. Michael Walden, " 'Don't Play Ball': Pro Sports Don't Drive the Economy," *Carolina Journal* 7, no. 2 (1997): 23.

3. Robert Baade, "Stadiums, Professional Sports, and Economic Development: Assessing the Reality" (policy study, The Heartland Institute, Chicago, Ill., April 4, 1994).

4. Gerald A. Carlino and N. Edward Coulson, "Should Cities Be Ready for Some Football?" *Business Review* (Federal Reserve Bank of Philadelphia) (2nd Quarter 2004): 7–17.

Chapter 36: Are We Running Out of Farmers, Farmland, and Soon, Food?

1. Comparison period is 1948 to 2001. Council of Economic Advisors, *Economic Report of the President, 2004*, Table B-100.
2. Comparison period is 1948 to 1999. Ibid., Table B-99.
3. Ibid., Table B-100.
4. Ibid., Tables B-99, B-100.

Chapter 37: Are Gas Prices at an All-Time High?

1. In 2003, a household earning between $30,000 and $40,000 spent 3.7% of their income on gasoline and motor oil. U.S. Bureau of Labor Statistics, *Consumer Expenditure Survey, 2003*.
2. The price adjustment uses the "core" consumer price index, which excludes price changes in the often volatile energy and food sectors.
3. Energy Information Agency, *Annual Energy Outlook 2005*, U.S. Department of Energy, Washington, D.C., February 2005, Figure 4.
4. David W. Meyer and Jeffrey H. Fischer, "The Economics of Price Zones and Territorial Restrictions in Gasoline Marketing" (working paper #271, Federal Trade Commission, Washington, D.C., March 2004), http://www.ftrc.gov/be/workingpapers/wp271.pdf.

Chapter 38: Do Big Oil Companies Manipulate Oil Supplies and Gas Prices?

1. Michael Burdette and John Zyren, "Gasoline Price Pass-Through," Energy Information Agency, U.S. Department of Energy, Washington, D.C., January 2003, http://www.eia.doe.gov/pub/oil_gass/petroleum/feature?articles/2003/gasoline pass/gasolinepass.htm.
2. Energy Information Agency, *Annual Energy Review, 2002*, U.S. Department of Energy, Washington, D.C., October 2003, Table 5.4.

Chapter 39: Should We Become Energy Self-Sufficient?

1. It should be remembered that electricity is not a "raw" fuel source. Instead, electricity must be generated from some other source of energy, such as coal, oil, nuclear power, or hydro power.
2. University of Florida, "Solar Power and Economics," http://www.plaza.ufl.edu/cvick.
3. "Shades of Green," *Consumer Reports* (December 2002): 62.
4. Hybrid vehicles may require battery pack replacements every eight years or 100,000 miles at a cost of $2,000, based on an analysis of Ford Escapes. Norihiko

Shirouzu and Jeffrey Bell, "Revolution under the Hood," *Wall Street Journal*, May 12, 2004, B1–B2.

5. Roger Segelken, "Ethanol Fuel from Corn Faulted as 'Unsustainable Subsidized Food Burning' in Analysis by Cornell Scientist," *Cornell News*, August 6, 2001, http://www.news.cornell.edu/releases/Aug01/corn-basedethanol.hrs.html.

6. Energy Information Agency, *Annual Energy Review, 2002*, Table 5.1.

7. Energy Information Agency, Office of Oil and Gas, "Petroleum Oil Production from the Coastal Plain of the Artic National Wildlife Refuge: Updated Assessment," Report #SR/O&G/2000-02, May 2000, http://www.eis.doe.gov/pub/oil_gas/petroleum/analysis_publications/artic_national_refuge/html.anwr10 1.html.

8. Jody M. Perkins, "Economic State of the U.S. Oil and Natural Gas Exploration and Production Industry: Long Term Trends and Recent Events" (American Petroleum Institute, Washington, D.C., April 30, 1999), 4.

9. The 12 cent per gallon security tax is from an analysis by Dr. Amy Myers Jaffee of the James A. Baker III Institute for Public Policy at Rice University. It is based on an assessment of the U.S. military costs directly related to sustaining the flow of oil from the Middle East (personal communication from Professor Jaffee). The higher estimate of 75 cents per gallon allocates half of the Defense Department budget to protecting imported Middle East oil.

Chapter 40: Is Immigration Hurting Our Economy?

1. U.S. Bureau of the Census, http://www.census.gov.

2. George Borjas, *Heaven's Gate* (Princeton, N.J.: Princeton University Press, 1999), 21.

3. Ibid., 23, 29.

4. Ibid., 86; and James P. Smith and Barry Edmonston, *The New Americans: Economic, Demographic, and Fiscal Effects of Immigration* (Washington, D.C.: National Academy Press, 1997), 173–253.

5. Borjas, *Heaven's Gate*, 91.

6. Ibid., 109.

7. Smith and Edmonston, *The New Americans*, 252–296.

8. Alan J. Auerbach and Philip Oreopoulos, "Generational Accounting and Immigration in the U.S." (working paper #7041, National Bureau of Economic Research, Cambridge, Mass., March 1999).

Chapter 42: Does It Take Two Incomes for Families to Get Ahead Today?

1. In married couple families in 2001, 50% of wives worked, compared to 25% in 1954. U.S. Bureau of the Census, *Statistical Abstract of the United States, 2003*,

no. 691 (Washington, D.C.: Government Printing Office, 2004); and U.S. Bureau of the Census, *Measuring Fifty Years of Economic Change*, Current Population Reports P60-203 (Washington, D.C.: Government Printing Office, September 1998), Table C-12.

2. U.S. Bureau of the Census, *Mini-Historical Statistics*, No. HS-12 (Washington, D.C.: Government Printing Office, 2005).

3. Unfortunately, published census data are not available to convert Figure 16 to a per person basis.

4. Anne E. Winkler, "Earnings of Husbands and Wives in Dual-Earner Families," *Monthly Labor Review* 121, no. 4 (1998): 42–48; and U.S. Bureau of the Census, *Statistical Abstract of the United States, 1995*, No. 240 (Washington, D.C.: Government Printing Office, 2005).

5. This concern is the theme of Elizabeth Warren and Amelia Warren Tyagi, *The Two Income Trap* (New York: Basic Books, 2003).

6. Michael L. Walden, "Absolute and Relative Consumption of Married U.S. Households in 1960 and 1996: The Cleavers Meet the Taylors," *Journal of Consumer Affairs* 36, no. 1 (2002): 77–98.

Chapter 43: Are Americans Drowning in Debt and Not Saving?

1. Includes mortgage debt and consumer credit debt. Council of Economic Advisors, *Economic Report of the President, 2004*, Tables B-75, B-77.

2. Ibid.

3. Ibid., Table B-30.

4. For a description of the *Survey of Consumer Finances*, see "Recent Changes in U.S. Family Finances: Evidence from the 1998 and 2001 Surveys of Consumer Finances," *Federal Reserve Bulletin* 89, no. 1 (2003): 1–32.

5. Medians are used for all averages in this chapter.

6. Angela C. Lyons, "How Credit Access Has Changed Over Time," *Journal of Consumer Affairs* 37, no. 2 (2003): 231–255.

7. The percentages are: 1989—8%; 1992—6%; 1995—7%; 1998—8%; 2001—7%. Federal Reserve System, *Survey of Consumer Finances* (Washington, D.C.: Board of Governors of the Federal Reserve System, various years).

8. Ibid.

9. The numbers are 7.8% in 2001 compared to 8.6% in 1989. Ibid.

10. The calculations and results are described in Richard Peach and Charles Steindel, "A Nation of Spend Thrifts: An Analysis of Trends in Personal and Gross Saving," *Current Trends in Economics and Finance* 6, no. 2 (2000): 1–6. An alternative measure, household net worth as a percentage of disposable income, averaged between 450% and 500% for the forty years from 1952 to 1992, after which it

steadily rose to 600%. Leonard Nakamura, "Investing in Intangibles: Is a Trillion Dollars Missing from GDP?" *Business Review* (Federal Reserve Bank of Philadelphia) (4th Quarter 2001): 27–37.

11. Michael L. Walden, *Economic Issues: Rhetoric and Reality* (Englewood Cliffs, N.J.: Prentice-Hall, 1995), 35.

12. Congressional Budget Office, *Baby Boomers' Retirement Prospects: An Overview* (Washington, D.C.: U.S. Government Printing Office, November 2003); Barbara Butrica and Cori Uccello, "How Will Boomers Fare at Retirement?" (AARP Public Policy Institute, Washington, D.C., #2004-05, May 2004).

Chapter 44: Do Women Earn Less Than Men?

1. U.S. Bureau of Labor Statistics, *Highlights of Women's Earnings in 2002*, Report 972 (Washington, D.C.: Government Printing Office, September 2003).

2. U.S. Department of Labor, Women's Bureau, *Time of Change: 1984 Handbook on Women Workers*, Bulletin 298 (Washington, D.C.: Government Printing Office, 1984).

3. U.S. General Accounting Office, *Women's Earnings* (Washington, D.C.: Government Printing Office, October 2003).

4. Daniel E. Hecker, "Earnings of College Graduates: Women Compared with Men," *Monthly Labor Review* 121, no. 3 (1998): 62–71.

5. Deborah A. Cobb-Clack and Yvonne Dunlop, "The Role of Gender in Job Promotions," *Monthly Labor Review* 122, no. 12 (1999): 32–38.

6. For more discussion of this point, see Francine D. Blau and Lawrence M. Kahn, "Gender Differences in Pay," *Journal of Economic Perspectives* 14, no. 4 (2000): 75–99.

Chapter 45: Are the Rich Getting Richer and Everyone Else Getting Poorer?

1. U.S. Census Bureau, *Income, Poverty, and Health Insurance Coverage in the United States, 2003*, Table A-3.

2. Thomas Piketty and Emmanuel Saez, "Income Inequality in the U.S.: 1913–1998," *Quarterly Journal of Economics* 118, no. 1 (1998): 1–40.

3. U.S. Census Bureau, *Income, Poverty, and Health Insurance Coverage in the United States, 2003*, Table A-3. The same trends are found in the majority of states. See Jared Bernstein, Heather Boushey, Elizabeth McNichol, and Robert Zahradnik, *Pulling Apart: A State-by-State Analysis of Income Trends* (Washington, D.C.: Center on Budget and Policy Priorities, Economic Policy Institute, April 2002), Tables 1, 4.

4. Alan Reynolds, "Musty Old Lies about Income Inequality," February 5, 2004, http://www.townhall.com.

Chapter 46: Is Poverty Getting Worse?

1. U.S. Census Bureau, *Income, Poverty, and Health Insurance Coverage in the United States, 2003*, Table 3.

2. See Chapter 40.

3. For more elaboration on this point, see Steven Camarota, *Importing Poverty: Immigration's Impact on the Size and Growth of the Poor Population in the United States*, Center Paper 15 (Washington, D.C.: Center for Immigration Studies, September 1999).

4. U.S. Bureau of the Census, *Statistical Abstract of the United States, 2003*, A82.

5. This also includes reducing money income by income and payroll taxes. U.S. Census Bureau, *Poverty in the United States, 2002*, Table 8.

6. W. Michael Cox and Richard Alm, *Myths of Rich and Poor* (New York: Basic Books, 1999), 15.

Chapter 48: Can Families Afford College?

1. U.S. Department of Education, National Center for Education Statistics, *Digest of Education Statistics, 2002*, Table 330, http://www.nces.ed.gov/programs/digest/.

2. Ibid.

3. Ibid.

4. The College Board, *Trends in College Pricing* (Washington, D.C.: College Entrance Examination Board, 2003), Table 5a.

5. Dennis Cauchon, "Tuition Burden Falls by a Third," *USA Today*, June 28, 2004, http://www.usatoday.com.

6. The College Board, *Trends in College Pricing*.

7. The $130,000 value is calculated in the following way: First, take the difference between a college graduate's salary in 2003 and a high school graduate's salary in 2003, and assuming a thirty-year work career, calculate the present value sum of the extra income for the college graduate. Second, convert the 1977 college and high school salaries to equivalent 2003 purchasing power dollar values, then perform the same calculation as in the first step. The $130,000 is the difference between the higher 2003 salary present value sum and the lower 1977 salary present value sum. Tuition values are from ibid. and U.S. Bureau of the Census, *Statistical Abstract of the United States, 2003*.

Chapter 49: Would Importing Drugs Lower Their Prices?

1. Based on comparing the consumer price index for prescription drugs and medical supplies to the overall consumer price index, 1990–2003, http://www.bls.gov.

2. There is some debate over exactly how much lower prescription drug prices

are in Canada compared to the United States. See Richard L. Manning, "Products Liability and Prescription Drug Prices in Canada and the U.S.," *Journal of Law and Economics* 41, no. 1 (1997): 203–243; and Congressional Budget Office, "Would Prescription Drug Importation Reduce U.S. Drug Spending?" (Economic and Budget Issue Brief, Washington, D.C., April 29, 2004).

3. John Carey, "A Cheap Fix? Not Really," *Business Week*, May 3, 2004, 52.

4. Paul Pecorino, "The Peculiar Economics of Importing Drugs from Canada," *Milken Institute Review* 6, no. 1 (2004): 35–41.

5. Statistics Canada, http://www.statcan.ca; and U.S. Department of Commerce, http://www.bea.doc.gov.

6. Congressional Budget Office, "Would Prescription Drug Importation Reduce U.S. Drug Spending?"; and Congressional Budget Office, "H.R. 2427: The Pharmaceutical Market Access Act of 2003" (CBO Cost Estimate, Washington, D.C., November 2003).

7. Tufts Center for the Study of Drug Development, *A Methodology for Counting Costs for Pharmaceutical R&D*, November 1, 2001, http://csdd.tufts.edu.

8. Jim Gilbert and Paul Rosenberg, "Addressing the Innovation Divide" (paper presented at the 2004 annual meeting of the Governors of the World Economic Forum for Healthcare, Davos, January 2004); and "The Trouble with Cheap Drugs," *The Economist*, January 31, 2004, 59.

9. U.S. Bureau of Labor Statistics, *Consumer Expenditure Survey, 2002*; statistic is for households over age sixty-five.

10. Ernst Berndt, "Pharmaceuticals in U.S. Health Care: Determinants of Quantity and Price," *Journal of Economic Perspectives* 16, no. 4 (2002): 45–66.

11. Ernst Berndt, Margaret Kyle, and Davina Ling, "The Long Shadow of Patent Expiration: Generic Entry and Rx to OTC Switches," in *Scanner Data and Price Indices*, ed. Robert Feestra and Matthew Shapiro (Chicago: University of Chicago Press, 2003), 229–267.

12. Richard G. Frank, "Prescription Drug Prices: Why Do Some Pay More Than Others Do?" *Health Affairs* 20, no. 2 (2001): 115–128.

Chapter 50: Can Government Lower Consumers' Health Costs?

1. Mark Sherman, "2003 Health Care Spending Up 7.8%," February 11, 2004, http://cbsnews.com.

2. As a percentage of U.S. gross domestic product, http://www.bea.doc.gov.

3. Uwe Reinhardt, Peter Hussey, and Gerald Anderson, "U.S. Health Care Spending in an International Context," *Health Affairs* 23, no. 3 (2004): 10–25.

4. Henry J. Aaron, "The Cost of Health Care Administration in the United States and Canada," *New England Journal of Medicine* 349, no. 8 (2003): 801–803.

5. Michael Walker, "Is Canadian Health Care a Good Model for the U.S. to Follow?" 2004, http://www.libertyhaven.com.

6. Nadeem Esmail and Michael Walker, "How Good Is Canadian Health Care? 2004 Report" (report, The Fraser Institute, Vancouver, British Columbia, Canada, April 2004).

7. For an elaboration of these recommendations, see Federal Trade Commission and U.S. Department of Justice, *Improving Health Care: A Dose of Competition* (Washington, D.C.: Government Printing Office, July 2004).

8. Ibid., Chapter 8, 2.

9. The implication is that health care is a luxury good, which means its consumption or use rises at a faster rate than income rises; see Campbell McConnell and Stanley Brue, *Economics: Principles, Problems, and Policies*, 16th ed. (Boston: McGraw-Hill, 2005), 677.

■ Index ■

Average tax burden, 51
Average tax rate, 53, 56

Bankruptcy, 151
Big business, 113
Budget deficits, 10
    and interest rates, 11
Business costs, 110–111
Business incentives, 43

Capital budget, 9
Capital gains, 152
Cartel, 131
Chief executive officers (CEOs)
    salary of, 122
College
    benefits from, 169
    financial aid, 167–168
    tuition, 167
Collusive oligopoly, 131
Comparative advantage, 94
Corporation, 65
Cost of living, 24
Cost/benefit framework, 45

Debt
    and family payments, 150
Deflation, 35
Demand, 103, 137
    law of, 176

Demand curve, 40
Demand side factors, 129
Discrimination, 153
Dividend and interest income, 68

Earned income tax credit, 38
Exchange rate, 102–104

Family debt, 148
Family size, 145
Federal Reserve, 47
Female-headed families, 160–161
Flat tax, 68
Food Stamps, 18
Foreign ownership, 101
Free agency, 121
Free lunch, 117
Friedman, Milton, 19

Gas
    and oil prices, 131
    price of, 127
Gasohol, 134
Generic drugs, 173
Gold standard, 34
Government spending, 4–5
Gross income, 55

Immigration
    benefits of, 131

government costs of, 132
  recent, 130, 160
  and Social Security, 132
  wage impact of, 131
Incentive, 106
Income
  after-tax, 141–142
  discretionary, 146
  and education, 145–146, 158
  family, 144–145
  federal tax on, 56
  inequality, 156
Inflation, 8, 11, 31, 34–35, 48, 104–105, 111, 127, 141, 148
Insourcing, 87–88
Instructional spending, 25
Interest rates, 10, 47
  long-term, 11
  real, 11, 111
  short-term, 11

Living wage, 37

Mandates
  health care, 177
  safety, 165
Marginal tax rate, 53, 56
Market segmentation, 172
Marriage tax penalty and bonus, 75
Medicaid, 18
Mercantilism, 99
Minimum wage, 37
Monopoly, 41
Movie stars
  salaries of, 120
Multiplier, 63, 116

National debt
  measurement of, 6–7
  ownership of, 7

Negative income tax, 19
Net worth
  family, 149
North American Free Trade Agreement (NAFTA), 89, 92–94

Occupations, 84–85
Oil
  price of, 130–131
Operating budget, 9
Opportunity cost, 21, 165–166
Output
  compared to inputs, 123
Outsourcing, 87–88

Personal savings rate, 148
Phelps, Edmund, 19
Poverty
  measures of, 161–162
Prescription drugs
  development of, 172
  importation of, 171–172
  price of, 171
  price controls on, 171–172
Price controls, 39–40
Price gouging, 40
Privatization, 16
Productivity, 81–82, 97, 124
Professional sports players
  salaries of, 120
Profit, 15, 39, 106–107, 110–111
Progressive tax, 52, 56, 70, 75–76
Proportional tax, 70
Purchasing power of the dollar, 3, 8

Real price, 127
Regressive tax, 70, 73

Sales tax, 71
School vouchers, 108
Security tax, 135

Service industry, 84
Shortage, 40
Single-payer health plan, 175
Social Security, 30–31, 138
   surplus, 27–28
   tax, 73
   transition issue, 32
Solar power, 133
Standard deduction, 76
Strong dollar, 102–103
Supply, 103, 137
Survey of Consumer Finances, 148–149

Tax bracket, 55, 57
Tax cut
   cost of, 60

Tax deduction, 57
Tax write-off, 57
Taxable income, 55
Trade deficit, 92, 99, 103
Trade surplus, 99, 103
Treasury securities, 7, 27–28, 31

Unit labor costs, 97

Waiting time
   and health care, 177
Waste, 107
Weak dollar, 102–103
Wind power, 133
World Trade Organization (WTO),
   89, 92–94

About the Author

MICHAEL L. WALDEN is Reynolds Distinguished Professor in the Department of Agricultural and Resource Economics, North Carolina State University, where he teaches courses in consumer economics, macroeconomics, microeconomics, and resource economics. He is the author of several books and over 200 academic articles, research monographs, conference presentations, and research reports on economic and consumer behavior. He writes and co-produces two radio programs, *The Economic Perspective* and *The Economic Focus*; writes the bi-weekly newspaper column, *You Decide*; and conducts public programs on issues of economic forecasting, behavior, and development.